P. Z. Lustic,
November, 1960.

THE TEMPLE OF JERUSALEM

STUDIES IN BIBLICAL ARCHAEOLOGY NO. 5

THE TEMPLE OF JERUSALEM

ANDRÉ PARROT

Curator-in-Chief of the French National Museums,
Professor at the Ecole du Louvre, Paris,
Director of the Mari Archaeological Expedition

SCM PRESS LTD
56 BLOOMSBURY STREET
LONDON

Translated by B. E. Hooke
from the French

LE TEMPLE DE JÉRUSALEM
(*Delachaux et Niestlé, Neuchâtel, Switzerland, 1954*)

First published in English 1957

Printed in Great Britain by
The Camelot Press Ltd., London and Southampton

CONTENTS

[5]

LIST OF ILLUSTRATIONS

FIGURES

List of Illustrations

Figures

(*All these illustrations are made from original or unpublished drawings*)

FOREWORD

One day in thy courts is better than a
thousand in my own house.

Ps. 84.10.

Of all the buildings in ancient Jerusalem none was
more impressive, none had a more remarkable
history than the Temple. For more than a thousand
years it had provided a permanent spiritual and
religious centre, witnessing to the real presence of
Yahweh among his people. Built by Solomon at the
height of his glory, it did not survive the Babylonian
assault in 586 B.C., when Nebuchadnezzar's armies
destroyed the holy city and led its people away into
captivity. 'By the rivers of Babylon' the exiles refused
to sing the songs of Zion in a strange land and turned
their gaze to the west, towards the shrine which,
though laid in ruins, was still the object of their
devotion.

But Babylon herself was to experience defeat, and
Cyrus the Achaemenid released the captives and
gave them permission, not only to return to their
country, but to rebuild their shattered city. The
reconstruction was not carried out without difficulty
and the restored Temple was only a faint reflection
of Solomon's magnificent building, and still less like

the Temple of Ezekiel's vision which he had promised to his people when the happier days of the restoration should come. It was the Idumean, Herod the Great, who at last put an end to the 'scandal' that Yahweh's house was meaner than those of his worshippers. In order to conciliate his subjects and induce them to forget his alien origin, the king, in his programme of public works, gave first place to religious and funerary buildings. What he had done at Hebron to honour the memory of Abraham, ancestor of the chosen people, there was far more reason to do at Jerusalem, and on an infinitely grander scale: to prepare for the God of the Promise a house worthy of his royal state. This was the Temple which Jesus knew and whose destruction he foretold. This shrine 'of magnificent stones' was to fall under the blows of the Romans in A.D. 70 at the time of the first Jewish rising. Its destruction was completed by the Emperor Hadrian, who, after his victory over Bar Cochba, erected a statue of himself, facing one of Jupiter, on the site where God had been worshipped for more than a thousand years. When in his turn the Caliph Omar came there in A.D. 638, he found, it is said, the whole place buried in debris. With his own hands he began the work of clearing it. Fifty years later the magnificent mosque of Abd-el-Melik was to stand upon the sacred rock.

But even then the vicissitudes of history were not ended: when the Crusaders captured Jerusalem in

1099 they transformed the mosque into a Christian church, the *Templum Domini*. But their occupation of the site was a brief one; in 1187 Saladin recaptured Jerusalem and replaced the Cross by the Crescent, which still dominates the platform and the shrine that today is wrongly named the 'Mosque of Omar'. How amazing is the persistence of 'holy places'! Religions may change, but their sites are changeless. What a dramatic and eventful history has unrolled since the day when King David purchased from Ornan the Jebusite a portion of land on which he built the first altar and dedicated it to Yahweh!

I

THE TEMPLE OF SOLOMON

It may seem strange that no shrine dedicated to Yahweh existed in Jerusalem before the time of Solomon. Having conquered the Canaanite city of the Jebusites, not without difficulty (II Sam. 5), David transferred his capital there from Hebron, strengthened the defences of the city and quickly set about building a palace for himself. For this enterprise he engaged the help of foreign workmen—carpenters and stonemasons—whom Hiram[1] King of Tyre sent him, together with cedar-wood, which was particularly plentiful in Phoenician Lebanon (II Sam. 5.11). David then brought back the ark, which had remained in the country of the Philistines after the disaster at Shiloh (I Sam. 4) and, after many vicissitudes, had been deposited in the house of Abinadab at Kiriath-Jearim (I Sam. 7.1; II Sam.

[1] According to Menander and Josephus, Hiram I reigned at Tyre from 968-935. He was contemporary with Solomon. It is possible, however, that the reference here is to his father, Abibaal. Father de Vaux, *Les Livres de Samuel*, p. 155, n. *a*, suggests 'either the name of Hiram has been added, or else this expedition took place later in David's reign'. (c. 1000 - c. 960)

6.2-3). The journey was made in two stages, and it was only after a stay of three months in the house of Obed-edom of Gath[1] that the ark entered 'the city of David, amid rejoicings' (II Sam. 6.12). It was placed in a tent and David made burnt offerings and peace-offerings 'before Yahweh' (6.17).

The contrast was glaring: King David residing in a palace of cedar-wood; the ark of Yahweh lodged in a tent (II Sam. 7.2). But this discrepancy persisted for a considerable time. The chroniclers give two different reasons for it. According to one version, David intended to build a 'house' for Yahweh, but Yahweh, speaking by the prophet Nathan, refused this mark of respect, declaring that since the Exodus from Egypt he had been content to move 'from tent to tent, from lodging to lodging' (II Sam. 7.6), and that he had never demanded for himself a 'palace of cedar-wood' (v. 7).[2]

According to another tradition (I Chron. 22), it was because David 'had shed much blood on the earth' (v. 8) that Yahweh would not allow him to build his house. However, the king made preparations for the work by collecting building material (vv. 3-4) and amassing considerable treasure (v. 14), which he placed in the care of his son Solomon,

[1] This was a Philistine with a pagan theophoric name (servant of Edom) belonging to the royal guard (cf. II Sam. 8.18, 15.18-20) who had become a worshipper of Yahweh.

[2] For the exegesis of II Sam. 7.1-17, as well as 1 Chron. 17, see *Bible du Centenaire*.

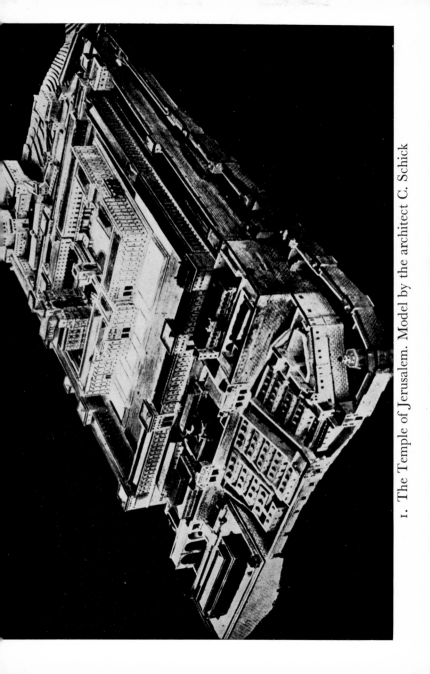

1. The Temple of Jerusalem. Model by the architect C. Schick

whose task it was to carry out what his father had not been permitted to accomplish.

King David, therefore, bound by this prohibition, could do no more than build an altar to Yahweh on a site indicated to him by God: a plot of land belonging to Ornan the Jebusite (II Sam. 24.18-25; I Chron. 21.18-22.1). David obeyed the instructions given to him, 'went up' to the appointed place and entered into legal possession of the land.[1] From that moment the site of the future temple was marked out and the location of the altar determined, very probably on the great rock[2] which is still to be seen today behind the grille and beneath the dome of the mosque of Abd-el-Melik.

*   *   *

After the death of his father David, and after having received the condolences of Hiram, king of Tyre,[3] Solomon determined to enlarge his capital. He chose the south side of the eastern hill, the peak of which (744 metres) overlooked the ancient city from a distance of about 20 metres (fig. I). There he proposed to construct a group of buildings worthy of his power and of the reputation which he hoped to acquire, not only within his own country, but also beyond its frontiers. Neither the trained workmen

[1] For a payment of 50 silver shekels, according to II Sam. 24.24; 600 gold shekels, according to I Chron. 21.25.

[2] It is possible that this rock had been originally the place of sacrifice of a Jebusite cult, but this cannot be proved.

[3] I Kings 5.1.

B

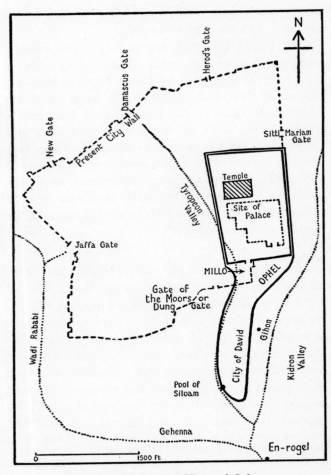

I. Jerusalem at the Time of Solomon

nor the necessary materials required to carry out these ambitious projects were to be found in Palestine. Solomon therefore entered into negotiations with Hiram and concluded an agreement with him[1] according to which Hiram was to provide not only timber (cedar and cypress) but skilled workmen, stonemasons and carpenters, to be recruited from Gebal, whence from the beginning of the third millennium Egypt had drawn its supplies.[2] It was agreed that in exchange Solomon should provide corn and oil, foodstuffs which Phoenicia had to import or, at all events, was glad to receive.

We do not propose to describe here the official residences and public buildings. Nevertheless, it should be remembered that within Solomon's great complex of buildings (fig. II) it is necessary to distinguish: the palace[3] (I Kings 7.8), the 'house of the forest of Lebanon'[4] (I Kings 7.2-5), the 'hall of

[1] I Kings 5.10-11, 18.

[2] The earliest Egyptian documents found at Gebal-Byblos date from the time of the Pharaoh Khasekhemui (Second Dynasty).

[3] The private residence seems to have been away from the main thoroughfare, as was the case in the palace of Mari. It must have been exceedingly large to be capable of housing the considerable royal harem: seven hundred princesses, three hundred concubines (I Kings 9.3).

[4] So called because of its cedar-wood pillars. The guard room (cf. the hundreds of gold bucklers mentioned in I Kings 10.16-17), arsenal (Isa. 22.8), repository of the 'treasure' (I Kings 10.21), which the kings sometimes showed to visitors (Isa. 39.2) and which they often plundered when they had to pay heavy tribute to exacting overlords: Ahaz to Tiglathpileser (II Kings 16.8), Hezekiah to Sennacherib (II Kings 18.15) to mention only two.

pillars'[1] (I Kings 7.6), the 'throne-room'[2] (I Kings

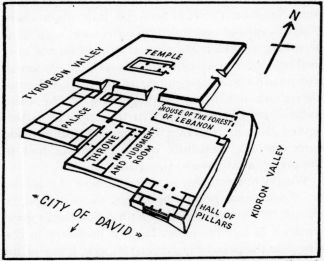

II. Solomonic Buildings. Sketch plan of the layout (based on Kurt Galling, Biblisches Reallexikon, *cols. 411–12)*

[1] From the mention of a portico and pillars 'on the front' (I Kings 6.6) it is possible to reconstruct this building after the pattern of the *bit hilani*, common in Hittite culture and North Syria.

[2] The finest ornament of this apartment must have been the gold and ivory throne (I Kings 10.18-20), placed on a dais approached by six steps. A number of ancient sculptures have served to throw light on the description which is given of it—for example, a relief on the sarcophagus of Ahiram, an ivory from Megiddo, etc., where a king is depicted seated on a throne flanked by sphinxes. 'Nothing like it had ever been made for any kingdom', says the scribe (I Kings 10.20)—a comment which recalls the inscription on the clasp of a necklace found by P. Montet at Tanis in the necropolis of the Psusennehs, contemporaries of Solomon: 'The King ordered a necklace of lapis to be made such as had never before been seen.'

7.7), where the king would give audiences and administer justice, and, finally, the 'house of Pharaoh's daughter'[1] (I Kings 7.8).

If the suggested reconstructions are accurate, there were two approaches to the Temple from the residences and public buildings: one used by the people of Jerusalem and by foreign visitors, and one reserved for the king, who could thus go directly from his private apartments to the 'house' which he had built for Yahweh. It is very probable that all these buildings were erected concurrently; nothing in the references in I Kings 7.1 and 9.10 excludes the possibility.

*   *   *

'In the four hundred and eightieth year after the children of Israel came out of the land of Egypt, in the fourth year of his reign, in the month Ziv, that is the second month, Solomon built the Temple for Yahweh' (I Kings 6.1).[2] If the exact date of the Exodus were known there would be no difficulty. Unfortunately, the chronology is still a matter of dispute,[3] and the dating of the Temple must be arrived at by other means.

[1] Probably an apartment within the palace.

[2] All exegetes agree that this verse is an editorial gloss. For example, Father Vincent (*RB*, 1907, p. 516); Father de Vaux, *Les Livres des Rois*, p. 43, n. *b*; *Bible du Centenaire* (note to I Kings 6.1). On the number 480 (40 × 12) see the very pertinent comments of J. Gray in *Vetus Testamentum*, IV (1954), p. 153.

[3] Canon E. Drioton stated the problem very clearly at the first

If W. F. Albright's dating of the death of Solomon in 923 B.C. is accepted, then the king, having reigned for forty years, would have ascended the throne in 963 B.C. The fourth year of his reign would then be the year 959 B.C., and the building of the Temple would have been begun at that date.[1] The work took seven years and five months, for the completion of it 'in the eleventh year, in the month Bul' is noted (I Kings 6.38).[2] Judging by the dimensions of the edifice, building proceeded slowly and must have been done with much care. Besides the foreign craftsmen already mentioned, Solomon secured the help of a Tyrian bronze-worker, a certain Hiram (I Kings 7.13-14), whose ability, skill, and knowledge are extolled.[3]

French Congress of Biblical Archaeology and Eastern Studies at Saint-Cloud, April 23, 1954.

[1] In a short study, 'The Date of the Founding of Solomon's Temple', *BASOR*, 119 (1950), pp. 20-2, M. B. Rowton supports this dating: according to Josephus, the Temple was begun in the twelfth year of Hiram's reign and one hundred and forty-five years before the founding of Carthage, which is assigned to 814 B.C. A simple addition (814+145=959) shows that the dates agree. E. R. Thiele in *Vetus Testamentum*, IV (1954), p. 191, takes a different view and does not accept Rowton's argument. These divergences sufficiently justify the use of the conditional tense.

[2] The month Ziv is April-May; Bul is October-November. Thus building began in the spring and finished in the autumn of the seventh year, before the rainy season.

[3] According to II Chron. 2.13, this craftsman was called Huram-abi. Gerard de Nerval, *Voyage en Orient*, III, pp. 180-335 (Imprimerie Nationale, 1950) gives the story of Hiram as related by story-tellers in the cafés of Constantinople during the nights of Ramadan. It is said also that Hiram invented freemasonry.

In spite of the very detailed information given in I Kings 6-7 and II Chron. 3-4,[1] the reconstruction of the Temple is still, in certain respects, a matter of conjecture, particularly since nothing of it remains. Moreover, comparisons drawn from Egypt and

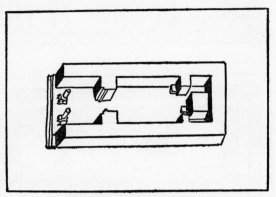

III. The Temple of Taïnat
(*from* BA, *IV, p. 21*)

Mesopotamia may be misleading. The most fruitful source of information would be a Phoenician temple of the tenth century B.C., but none has come to light. The shrine of Taïnat (fig. III) in Upper Syria, between Aleppo and Antioch, has been cited as a possible pattern; it dates from the ninth century B.C.

[1] In addition to critical editions, the reader should consult the very detailed study by Father Vincent, 'La description du Temple de Solomon', in *RB*, 1907, pp. 515-42, in which constant use is made of archaeological sources. On the sources used by the Chronicler, see A. M. Brunet, in *RB*, 1954, pp. 354-68.

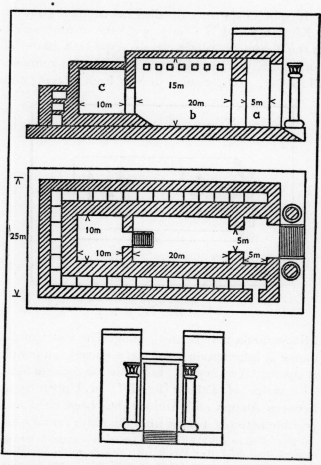

IV. The Temple of Solomon (*from Watzinger,*
Denkmäler Palästinas)

and shows the tripartite division.[1] In any case, it is clear that every possible use should be made of archaeological material from the western Semitic world, without, however, neglecting Egypt, with which Solomon's relations were sufficiently close for a daughter of Pharaoh to have entered his harem.

It is clear that all the reconstructions attempted in the nineteenth century or at the beginning of the twentieth should be treated with extreme caution.[2] One of them is reproduced here (Pl. 1), but simply as a historical document, for nowadays little value is attached to such models, their principal defect being that they combine a number of incompatible elements, without any regard for chronology.

The Temple (fig. IV) was essentially a rectangular building erected on a platform,[3] orientated east and west, and consisting of a porch (*ulâm* or *elâm*) and two chambers, one behind the other (*hekâl* and *debîr*). The external measurements are given in cubits (1 cubit being approximately 50 centimetres or 20 in.).[4]

*   *   *

[1] In *The American Journal of Archaeology*, 1937, p. 9, fig. 4; W. F. Albright, *Archaeology and the Religion of Israel*, p. 143; G. E. Wright, 'Solomon's Temple Resurrected', in *The Biblical Archaeologist*, IV (1941), pp. 20-1; A. G. Barrois, *Manuel d'archéologie biblique*, II, p. 443.

[2] The most recent is that of Stevens in *BA*, XVIII (1955), p. 42. But the battlemented walls are very doubtful.

[3] Based on the reference in Ezek. 41.8.

[4] See references to the Temple in works by I. Benzinger, *Hebräische Archäologie*, pp. 215-19; C. Watzinger, *Denkmäler Palästinas*, I, pp.

The porch (*ulâm* or *elâm*)[1] was a kind of entrance hall (*a*) either projecting[2] or flush with the building itself.[3] It corresponds to the porch or narthex in a Christian church. It was entered through double doors and was 20 cubits (*c*. 10 m.) wide and 10 cubits (*c*. 5 m.) in depth; its height is not known.[4] Two bronze pillars are placed in front of the porch (I Kings 8.15-22; II Kings 25.17; II Chron. 3.15-17, 4.12-13; Jer. 52.17-23). Their shafts were 18 cubits (9 m.) high, surmounted by capitals 5 cubits (2½ m.) in height, of elaborate design, wide at the base and opening out into a lotus or lily form adorned with bronze festoons and garlands of pomegranates. These columns, 4 cubits (*c*. 2 m.) in diameter and some 12 m. high, stood either side of the entrance, supporting nothing. Each had a name: the one on the right (south) side was *Jachin*, the one on the left (north) was *Boaz* (I Kings 7.21).

How are these to be interpreted? The obelisks of Egyptian temples, the stone pillars of the high places, the pairs of pillars erected at the entrance to many

436-45; also the study by G. E. Wright, 'Solomon's Temple Resurrected', in *BA*, IV, pp. 17-31. For other studies—for example, those by Moehlenbrink, Scott, L. Waterman—see Bibliography.

[1] In Assyrian *ellamu*—what is in front.

[2] Benzinger, *Bible du Centenaire, Bible de Jérusalem*.

[3] Watzinger (followed here), Wright, Barrois.

[4] The figure of 120 cubits, given in II Chron. 3.4, seems to be greatly exaggerated, for the first chamber was not more than 30 cubits high. This is the figure used here.

oriental shrines—Khorsabad, Tyre, Hierapolis[1]—
have all at one time or another been offered for
consideration. It has also been suggested that they
were huge incense-burners or torch-holders,[2] or
even permanent indicators for calculating the
equinoxes.[3] Nor have symbolic interpretations been
lacking: the two pillars between which the sun rises
in the east; trees of life; the pillars of cloud and fire
which went with the Israelites in the wilderness, etc.

There is the same lack of certainty about the
meaning of the names. The following have been
suggested:

He (Yahweh) will establish (*yakin*) with power
(*boaz*) the column or the temple;

May [God] keep [it] upright by [his] power;[4]

[1] The baked earth model of the Cypriot Temple of Dali (in the
Louvre, Room XVI of the Department of Oriental Antiquities) has
sometimes, erroneously, been cited. In this monument pillars surmounted by floral capitals support an architrave. To the other
examples mentioned may be added *Sit Shamshi*, found at Susa, where
there are two pillars, one on each side of the table of offerings
(reproduction in *Ziggurats et Tour de Babel*, Pl. III).

[2] W. F. Albright, 'Two Cressets from Marisa and the Pillars of
Jachin and Boaz', in *BASOR*, 85 (1942), pp. 18-27; H. G. May,
'The two Pillars before the Temple of Solomon', in *BASOR*, 88
(1942), pp. 19-27.

[3] J. Morgenstern, in *Hebrew Union College Annual*, XXI (1948),
pp. 471-4. According to Dussaud in *Syria*, XXXII (1955), p. 127,
G. Ryckmans considers that the pillars 'commemorate the names
of two fortresses renowned for Israelite victories'. J. L. Myres (*Book
List*, 1955, p. 18) does not regard the pillars as separate from the
building.

[4] Interpretation offered by E. Renan, *Histoire du peuple d'Israël*, II,
p. 143. According to him they are 'talismanic inscriptions' written
on the columns by the Phoenician metal-workers.

[27]

He will confirm strength in him.

He (Solomon) established [this column] with power;

Boaz set it up.[1]

R. B. Y. Scott[2] has suggested that the two words might be the first words of dynastic oracles inscribed on the pillar and would mean:

Yahweh will *establish* his throne for ever! Let the king rejoice in the *strength* of Yahweh!

Clearly numerous unsolved problems meet us even at the entrance to the Temple. It may be recalled that the two columns were still standing when Jerusalem was taken by Nebuchadnezzar in 586 B.C. The Babylonians broke them up and carried the pieces away (II Kings 25.13).[3] But the memory of them persisted. They may still be seen portrayed on a fragment of glass found in the catacombs in Rome (fig. V).[4] But no representation which has yet

[1] This hypothesis would seem to be untenable, since the Phoenician bronze-worker who set up the columns is known to have been Hiram (I Kings 7.21).

[2] R. B. Y. Scott, 'The Pillars Jachin and Boaz', in *JBL*, LVIII (1939), pp. 143 *et seq.*

[3] Such an episode was often represented on Assyrian reliefs—for example, the sack of the temple of Musasir by the troops of Sargon II on a stone slab from Khorsabad.

[4] Numerous reproductions are to be found in the textbooks: Gressmann, *AOB*, fig. 504; Benzinger, *Hebräische Archäologie*, fig. 224; Perrot and Chipiez, *Histoire de l'Art*, IV, p. 293. It came from a Jewish tomb of the third or fourth century A.D. W. Baumgartner (*Neue Zürcherzeitung*, 19, XII, 1954) suggests, however, that the glass fragment may represent the coffer containing the Torah.

been found is more remarkable than that to be seen on a *naos*[1] from the neighbourhood of Tyre (Burdj-esh-Shemali), now in the museum at Beirut, and which is probably the first to be noted in connection

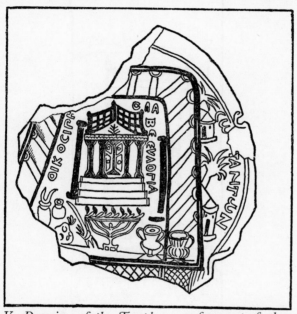

V. Drawing of the Temple on a fragment of glass from the Catacombs (from Perrot and Chipiez, HGA, IV, p. 293)

[1] A *naos* dating from the fifth century B.C., published by M. Chehab in *Berytus*, I (1934), p. 44 and Pl. XI, 1. To this must now be added the 'model of the sanctuary' discovered at Far'ah in 1954 by Father de Vaux. (*RB*, 1955, pp. 571-2, Pl. XIII): this dates from the ninth century B.C.

with the Temple: on the façade of what must be the
temple of Melqart at Tyre are to be seen two
detached pillars supporting nothing (fig. VI). These

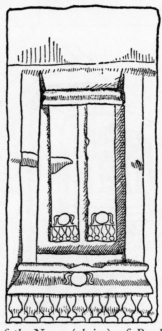

VI. Pillars of the Naos *(shrine) of Burdj esh-Shemali*
(from M. Chehab, in Berytus, *I (1934) Pl. XI, I)*

might well be the pillars Jachin and Boaz of Solomon's shrine.

* * *

From the porch, double doors of cypress-wood

(I Kings 6.34) gave entrance to the *hekâl*,[1] a word which has been variously rendered 'temple', 'great chamber', 'hekal' (the last preserving the Hebrew form).

This is sometimes called the 'holy place', to distinguish it from the 'most holy place', the *debîr* or inner chamber (see below, p. 33). The *hekâl* was a rectangular room, 40 cubits (*c.* 20 m.) long, 20 cubits (*c.* 10 m.) wide, 30 cubits (15 m.) high,[2] panelled throughout with cedar-wood, and decorated with carvings of cherubim, palms (palmettos), and garlands of flowers (I Kings 6.29); the same collection of motifs may be seen in the Phoenician and Syrian ivories found in a number of excavated sites at Ras Shamra, Megiddo, Samaria, Arslan Tash, Nimrud, and Khorsabad (fig. VII). The building was lit by arches[3] cut in the upper part of the walls (I Kings 6.4), very probably similar to those represented on the ivories (fig. VIII) known

[1] Cf. the Assyrian *ekallu*=palace, from the Sumerian *e-gal* (great house).

[2] The 'throne-room' (No. 65) of the palace of Mari, which certainly formed part of a religious building on the same kind of plan (two communicating chambers), was 25 m. long, 10 m. wide, and between 10 m. and 15 m. in height. The Greek text has 25 cubits high, instead of the 30 cubits of the Hebrew text.

[3] The translation of this passage presents difficulties: Father Vincent renders it 'windows with grilled sashes'; Father de Vaux, 'windows with frames and grilles'; *Bible du Centenaire*, 'windows closed by a wooden trellis'; Segond, 'windows with strong grilles'; Goodspeed, 'windows with narrow frames'; R.V. 'windows of fixed lattice work'.

VII. *Motifs of Syro-Phoenician Ivories:* 'Cherubims' *and frieze of flowers* (*from Thureau-Dangin*, Arslan Tash, *Pls. XXXI, XLVI*)

VIII. *Syro-Phoenician Ivories found at Arslan Tash:* (*a*) *The* 'Woman at the Window'; (*b*) *Goddesses guarding Horus*

2. The site of the Haram esh-Sherif, from the West

as 'the woman at the window'[1], which seem to be built up from several wooden frames.

In the *hekâl* were the various cult objects (I Kings 7.48-50): a gold altar (for incense), the table of the shewbread,[2] ten candelabra[3] (five on the left, five on the right), and various utensils—lamps, goblets, cups, knives, basins, braziers—such as were to be found in all shrines where a sacrificial cult was practised, and which constituted valuable booty if the place was looted.

*   *   *

The *hekâl* led directly into the *debîr* (I Kings 6.19-20).[4] This chamber was a perfect cube—20 cubits (*c.* 10 m.) in length, breadth, and height. This was the *Holy of holies* or *most holy place* (I Kings 6.19-20). Segond translates it 'sanctuary', the *Bible du Centenaire* and Goodspeed 'inner room', the *Bible de Jérusalem* retains the Hebrew word *debîr*, R.V. gives 'oracle'. Was this holy of holies on the same level as the *hekâl* or was it approached by a stair? (Watzinger and Vincent). The second supposition is probably to be preferred.[5]

[1] Wright, in *BA*, IV (1941), p. 26.

[2] This is certainly the 'altar of cedar-wood' plated with gold of I Kings 6.20.

[3] These candelabra are not to be confused with the seven-branched lampstand which did not exist before the return from the exile.

[4] From the root *dbr*, Arabic *dubr*=what is behind.

[5] There was the same arrangement in the palace at Mari in the hall of audience where we found a 'raised chapel' (*Syria*, XVIII (1937), p. 69).

c

There is no mention of any window and, since the entrance was closed with folding doors (I Kings 6.31), no light would have entered except when the doors were open, which would have been only rarely. But Yahweh had declared that he 'would dwell in darkness' (I Kings 8.12), and it is clear that, under the symbol of the ark, he himself was present in this mysterious chamber.

In fact it was there that 'the ark of the law of Yahweh' (I Kings 6.19) had been placed—the real palladium of the nation, symbol of the actual presence of God in the midst of his people. On either side of it were cherubim of olive-wood plated with gold, 10 cubits (*c.* 5 m.) high and with a wing span of 10 cubits. We are told that the wing-tip of one touched the wall, and that of the other touched the opposite wall, while their other wings met in the middle of the chamber (I Kings 6.27).[1] One other indication of the position of the cherubim is preserved (I Kings 8.6-7; II Chron. 5.7-8) where it is clearly stated that the wings covered the ark and its poles. This indication justifies the reconstruction shown in fig. IX.[2]

Here the cherubim[3] seem to perform the function

[1] The same description is given in II Chron. 3.10-13, but in a more elaborate form.

[2] This is Gressmann's reconstruction, combining two drawings (Gressmann, *AOB*, fig. 391, and Benzinger, *Hebräische Archäologie*, p. 314, fig. 401).

[3] On the subject of the cherubim see the philological and archaeological study by Dhorme and Vincent in *RB*, 1926, pp. 328-58, 481-99.

of guardians, after the model of those which watched over the tree of life in the 'garden of Paradise' (Gen. 3.24), but the imagery is probably derived from Egypt. Egyptian sphinxes and tutelary goddesses,

IX. *The 'cherubim' above the Ark (from Gressmann, in Benzinger,* Hebräische Archäologie, *p. 314, with some slight modifications)*

spreading their wings over the infant Horus (fig. VIII), were to become part of the Syro-Phoenician art forms, and at that time Palestine had much closer relations with Egypt than with Mesopotamia.

It is not possible here to discuss in detail the problem of the ark, which has long been a matter of dispute, and concerning which the most varied theories have been propounded.[1] It would seem that

[1] The short account by Kurt Galling, *Biblisches Reallexikon,* cols. 343-4, is very useful. See below, Bibliography, p. 108.

in this matter there was some development in the thought of the Israelites themselves. According to some traditions, very clearly stated, the ark was a military palladium, to which recourse was had in difficult situations, in the belief that the intervention of Yahweh himself could thereby be secured. This is what happened at the Battle of Aphek, for instance. The ark, which at that time was deposited in the sanctuary at Shiloh, was carried into battle (I Sam. 4.3-4) and the Philistines spoke the truth when, on learning of its presence, they declared 'A god has come into the camp' (v. 7). Nevertheless the Israelites were defeated and the ark was captured.

Is it possible to form any idea of the appearance of the ark? Some have suggested that it was shaped like a throne, on the evidence of certain texts[1] and of monuments discovered in Phoenicia on which is represented the empty seat of a god flanked by cherubim (fig. X).[2] According to other scholars it was a small-scale model of a shrine or altar, similar to the pottery models found during excavations at Megiddo.[3] Whatever its shape, Yahweh was enthroned or dwelt there, in truth, though invisibly.

[1] 'The ark of God which bears the name of Yahweh of hosts, enthroned on the cherubim' (II Sam. 6.2; cf. I Sam 4.4; I Chron. 13.6).

[2] *Syria*, V (1924), Pl. 32. A throne dedicated to Astarte in the museum at Beirut.

[3] H. G. May, 'The Ark. A Miniature Temple', in *AJSL*, LII (1936), pp. 215-34; H. G. May and R. M. Gordon, *Material Remains of the Megiddo Cult*, Pls. XIII-XV.

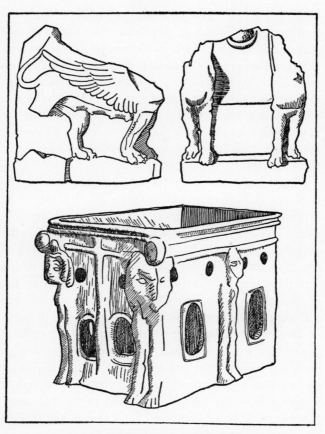

X. (a) Throne dedicated to Astarte
   (b) Altar at Megiddo

Since then the ark was his permanent and yet mobile abode, it is not surprising that Israel should make use of this real presence to influence the military fortunes of the nation. David used it thus on several occasions and the ark went with the troops during his campaign against Ammon (II Sam. 9.11), and again when the king fled from Jerusalem at the time of Absalom's revolt (II Sam. 15.24-9). However, the king changed his mind and had the sacred chest carried back to the capital.

Side by side with the concept of the ark as the national palladium, there developed the notion of a receptacle for the Tables of the Law (I Kings 9.9; Deut. 10.1-5); this tradition was adopted by the priestly writer and from it arose the name 'Ark of the Law' or 'of the Covenant'[1] which is used in the latest Pentateuchal sources. These also testify to the presence of the cherubim, but place them in positions different from those indicated in the Book of Kings.[2]

The ark remained in its place in the Temple of Jerusalem for more than three hundred years. It does not appear that any hand was laid on it during the various crises which the land suffered, when the kings had to make inroads into their stores of treasure —secular or sacred—to meet the exactions of foreign conquerors—the Pharaoh Shishak (I Kings 14.26), Ben-hadad, king of Damascus (I Kings 15.18),

---

[1] Some translations give 'ark of the covenant' and 'ark of witness'.
[2] Cf. for example Ex. 25.18-20 and I Kings 6.27.

Joash, king of Israel (II Kings 14.14), Tiglathpileser the Assyrian (II Kings 16.8). The ark is indeed mentioned at the time of Josiah (621 B.C.) on the occasion of the reform of the cult, with which the name of the king of Judah is associated. This is its last official appearance. There is no mention of it in connection with the sack of the Temple by the Babylonians in 586 B.C. (II Kings 25.13-15). Very probably it had been removed beforehand, in the hope that it might be concealed in some safe place. It has been suggested that Jeremiah had some part in this, and that the ark might have been hidden in a cave in Mount Nebo.[1] Parker's expedition, about 1910, in fact made a search for it, only to come to a tragic end. But even if the ark had been put in 'a safe place', is it possible that its timber could have lasted until the present time[2], or that its plating would have escaped the greed of thieves?

The interior decoration of the shrine was equally rich. There is mention of carved woodwork everywhere (gourds, garlands of flowers, cherubim, palm-trees). There was the same decoration on the leaves of the folding doors (cherubim, palm-trees, and flowers), overlaid with gold plating (I Kings

[1] The story is given in II Mac. 2.4-6.

[2] Recent discoveries in the desert of Judaea have provided remarkable evidence of how perishable materials may be preserved in certain conditions, which, however, are not found everywhere in Palestine or Transjordan. Miss K. M. Kenyon's finds at Jericho also have revealed funeral furniture from the Bronze Age in a remarkable state of preservation: *ILN*, October 3, 1953, and July 24, 1954.

6.32,35). Even if allowance is made for exaggeration[1] in the high-flown style of the time[2] it is probable that gold was extensively used in the interior decoration of the holy place, since, according to the custom of the East, the use of the precious metal—symbol of wealth and power[3]—was not stinted. And Solomon had no lack of it.[4]

*   *   *

The roof of the Temple was certainly flat. It is highly unlikely that there were hollow spaces between the ceiling and the roof[5], still less probably a dome or vaulting. A strong framework of cedar-wood,[6] attached to the walls and held in place by

[1] Father de Vaux agrees with this view (see *Livres des Rois*, p. 46, n. *b*.) which is confirmed by the evidence of a number of Seleucid tombs at Mari (*Syria* XLI, 1955).

[2] I Kings 6.22, 30; II Chron. 3.5-7.

[3] At Mari, during the excavation of the temples of Shamash, Ishtar and Ninni-Zaza, the author on several occasions found fragments of gold leaf which must have come from woodwork, doors, or chests.

[4] The importing of gold is frequently mentioned in the Book of Kings; in one reference the value is given as 666 talents a year (I Kings 10.14-15). The Queen of Sheba also brought gold.

[5] On the model of Syrian temples of the Hellenistic or Roman era. Father Vincent, however, takes a different view; see *RB*, 1907, p. 523, n. 9.

[6] The text here is very obscure, the meaning of two words being uncertain. The *Bible du Centenaire* renders it: 'And he covered it with a ceiling of cedar-wood beams'. Father Vincent: 'he covered it with coffers and beams of cedar'; Father de Vaux: 'he covered the Temple with cedar'; (R.V.: 'He covered the house with beams and planks of cedar'; *International Critical Commentary*: rafters and *coffers*').

slings, supported a flat roof of beaten earth, which was remade and repaired every year before the rainy season.[1]

The main structure was built up of hewn stones—the only material with which Jerusalem was amply supplied—and stone was used for the foundations (I Kings 5.17) reinforced with wooden beams (I Kings 7.12). Evidence of this method of building has been found at a number of sites in the Eastern Mediterranean basin—at Ras Shamra (Phoenicia) and Egea.[2]

It is understandable that this technique should have been adopted and followed at Jerusalem, for Solomon had engaged Phoenician craftsmen and we are explicitly told that to the Giblites was assigned the double task of cutting and laying in place the timber and the stone (I Kings 5.18).

*   *   *

On three sides of the Temple (north, west and south) were attached additional structures, apparently enclosed between two walls (I Kings 6.5).[3]

[1] Evidence for this procedure was found in the architecture of the palace at Mari, and it is still common in the East.

[2] This has been confirmed by finds at Mari in buildings of unbaked brick—for example, the Assyrian ziggurat (*Syria*, XXI, 1940, p. 24 and fig. XVII).

[3] On this subject, see a number of studies by L. Waterman, 'The Damaged "Blue-prints" of the Temple of Solomon', in *JNES*, II (1943), pp. 284-94; 'The Treasuries of Solomon's Private Chapel', *JNES*, VI (1947), pp. 161-3; G. E. Wright (*JNES*, VII (1948), p. 53) disagrees with Waterman's conclusions; Waterman's reply, 'A Rebuttal', in *ibid.*, pp. 54-5, is not very convincing.

From the outside the wall of the Temple presented the appearance of a stairway with three levels (fig. IV); these served as supports for the rafters which joined another wall. Thus the whole structure consisted of a ground floor and two stories. On account of the setting back of the interior wall, the width of the ground floor was 5 cubits (*c.* 2 m. 50 cm.), that of the first floor was 6 cubits (3 m.), and that of the second 7 cubits (3 m. 50 cm.) (I Kings 6.6). The entrance was 'on the right', that is, the south side. Stairways (or trap-doors) led to the upper stories (I Kings 6.8), the height of the whole being 15 cubits (7 m. 50 cm.).

It is generally supposed that these additional buildings were for the use of the priests and Temple servants, but they served also as shops, storehouses, and storage space, such as all Eastern temples had. The 'treasure' was more probably deposited within the sanctuary, in the area of the *debîr*, possibly in convenient hiding-places underground or in the walls.[1] Nevertheless, some of these additional buildings may well have been intended to house the great quantity of valuable offerings belonging to Yahweh and therefore kept in his house.

*   *   *

The Temple was separated from the Palace, but the

[1] This was certainly the case at Mari, where in one of the shrines of the palace a concealed treasure chest came to light, but unfortunately it was empty (*Syria*, XIX (1938), Pl. VI, 4).

space surrounding it was not empty; various accessories connected with the cult were grouped there, which we shall now describe. A bronze altar, dating from the time of Solomon, is mentioned in I Kings, 8.64 and 9.25, but strangely enough no description of it is given in the Book of Kings.[1] In Chronicles, however, the dimensions are specified: length, 20 cubits (*c*. 33 ft. 4 in.); width, 20 cubits (33 ft. 4 in.); height, 10 cubits (16 ft. 8 in.) (II Chron. 6.1). The priests who went up to lay the burnt offerings on it would have to approach it by steps.[2]

The site of this altar is not indicated. It might have been on the rock of Ornan[3] or more probably beside it,[4] according to the account given of the dedication of the Temple. On the occasion of this ceremony so many sacrifices were offered that the bronze altar proved to be too small and Solomon had to 'consecrate the middle of the court' in order to provide a place of sacrifice (I Kings 8.64). The great rock which thrusts up through the ground in this area would seem to be particularly suitable for the purpose.[5]

In this matter the kings had a certain freedom of

[1] This should be placed between I Kings 7.22 (bronze columns) and 7.23 (bronze bath), following the order of items in II Chron. 2.17-4.1-2.

[2] As would have been necessary for the altar described in Ezek. 43.17, thus, as has been noted, contradicting the prescriptions of the Book of the Covenant, Ex. 20.26.

[3] Barrois, *Manuel*, II, p. 454.

[4] A. Lods, *Bible du Centenaire*, note to I Kings, 8.64.

[5] The dimensions of the rock are 17 m. 70 cm. by 13 m. 50 cm.

action, the best example of which is provided by Ahaz (736-716 B.C.). He had gone to Damascus to make his submission to the Assyrian king Tiglath-pileser and, having seen there the altar in the temple of the god Hadad, he sent the measurements and a model of it to Jerusalem, commanding Urijah, the high-priest, to have one made exactly like it (II Kings 16.10-11). When Ahaz returned to Jerusalem, his first action was to offer sacrifice on the new altar and to have the old one removed, adding the enigmatic and somewhat pompous words: 'As for the bronze altar, it will be necessary for me to take thought' (II Kings 16.15). But it seems likely that he had already taken thought, and that in fact Ahaz had submitted to the exactions of his overlord and his demands for the usual tribute.[1]

The platform. The only information is in II Chron. 6.12-13, where the measurements of the bronze pedestal are given: length, 5 cubits (2 m. 50 cm.); width, 5 cubits (2 m. 50 cm.); height, 3 cubits (1 m. 50 cm.). We are told that during the dedication ceremony, Solomon stood on it, and even knelt on it (II Chron. 6. 13).[2] Archaeology has preserved

---

[1] In the author's view, this is quite definitely implied in the account of what Ahaz did to this court and in connection with other cult objects (II Kings 16.17) which will be discussed below.

[2] According to I Kings 8.22, the king was *standing*, but a *kneeling* position is mentioned in I Kings 8.54. Some scholars see here an editorial gloss. There is archaeological evidence for both positions, but the former is much more common. There are also instances of persons being *seated* before the god (statues of the minister Ebih-il at

representations of similar platforms. Thus, on the stele of Baal the Thunderer from Ras Shamra[1] a figure is shown standing upright on a pedestal before the god, but with his back turned to him, and his right hand raised, and this is clearly the king.[2]

Numerous theories have been advanced as to the purpose of this platform; was it in order that the voice of the celebrant might carry as far as possible, or in order that he might be nearer, symbolically, to the god? The first is the simplest, and probably the best, explanation.

The bronze sea[3] (I Kings 7.23-6; II Chron. 4.2-5). This was a huge water tank resting on twelve oxen, placed in four groups of three at the four cardinal points (fig. XI). This enormous basin, decorated on its outer side with gourds, was 10 cubits (5 m.) in diameter and 5 cubits (2 m. 50 cm.) high, and held 2,000 *baths*.[4] It was filled with water and 'placed at

Mari, of Cudea at Lagash) and King David is said to have adopted this posture on occasions (II Sam. 7.18).

[1] C. F. A. Schaeffer, *Ugaritica*, II, Pl. XXIII.

[2] W. F. Albright, *Archaeology and the Religion of Israel*, third edition (1953), p. 158, mentions other examples of identical arrangements, previously noted by H. Schäfer and M. Müller.

[3] Literally, the sea of *molten metal*, generally translated *sea of bronze* or *sea of brass*.

[4] 3,000 according to II Chron. 4.5. The difference is explained, possibly a little too ingeniously, by C. C. Wylie, 'On King Solomon's Molten Sea', in *BA*, XII (1949), p. 90. The equivalent in modern measures is given variously by different authors. Benzinger and the *Bible du Centenaire* give 72,880 litres (16,040 gallons), but the *Bible de Jérusalem* gives 'about 45,000 litres' (9,905 gallons), which seems preferable. This applies to the 2,000 *baths*.

the right side of the Temple to the south-east'
(I Kings 7.39) for the ablutions of the priests (II
Chron. 4.6). It was not very easy of access, and it
would seem that there was another, and symbolic,
reason for it. The 'sea of bronze' might suggest

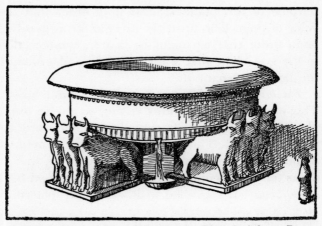

*XI. The Bronze Sea of Solomon's Temple (from Perrot
and Chipiez, HGA IV, p. 327)*

either the sacred lake of Egyptian temples or the
Babylonian *apsu*—the mass of 'waters beneath the
earth'.[1] It has also been suggested that this vessel
might represent the heavenly ocean supported by
twelve bulls corresponding to the twelve signs of the
zodiac. But Weidner has pointed out that the first

[1] The exact words of Ex. 20.4.

[46]

Babylonian zodiac had seventeen,[1] not twelve, signs, which invalidates this interpretation. It seems probable that the twelve oxen (=bulls) were both symbolic and decorative. As is well known, the bull, in the Canaanite world, was the type of fertility, and the four groups of three were so placed for the purpose of orientation (I Kings 7.25).[2]

The great basin remained in this position until the reign of Ahaz (736-716 B.C.). On his return from Damascus, the king of Judah, among other things, 'had the bronze sea removed from the oxen on which it rested, and placed on a stone pavement' (II Kings 16.17). There is little doubt that he did this because he needed the metal for the tribute demanded by the king of Nineveh.

The best archaeological find which may be compared with the sea of bronze is the great basin of Amathus, found in Cyprus and now in the Louvre. Hewn from a single block of fairly soft limestone, it measures 2 m. 20 cm. in diameter and is 1 m. 85 cm. in height. Four imitation handles are carved on the edge of the basin, each with the figure of a bull within it.

The moveable lavers. These were ten bowls set on stands fitted with wheels. The description given in

[1] *AFO*, VII (1931), pp. 170-8, quoted by Albright, *ARI*, p. 217, n. 74.

[2] The suggestion sometimes made that *four* seasons are represented cannot be accepted, because in the East there are actually only two: summer and winter. This is correctly indicated in Gen. 8.22.

I Kings 7.27-9,[1] though very detailed, presents great difficulties on account of a number of technical terms, the meaning of which is far from clear. Any reconstruction is therefore highly conjectural (fig.

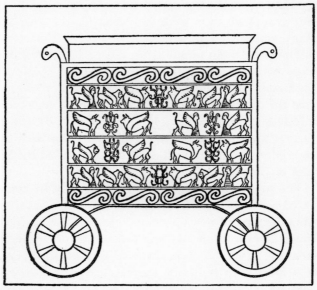

XII. Moveable Laver of Solomon's Temple (from Gressmann, AOTB, No. 508, with modifications)

XII). The bronze stands were decorated with a whole collection of beasts—evidently symbolic (bulls, lions, cherubim)—and various vegetal or linear motifs (palm-trees, scrolls). On these square stands

[1] In II Chron. 4.6 there is simply a list.

(4 cubits, or 2 m. in length and width, 3 cubits or
1 m. 50 cm. high) were set bowls, 4 cubits in diameter,
each one holding 40 *baths*.[1]

In view of the textual difficulties, any reconstruction has to depend on archaeological data. In fact,

*XIII. Lavers from Larnaka and Enkomi (from Benzinger,
op. cit., p. 219)*

in Cyprus, at Enkomi and Larnaka, two bowls have
been found,[2] much smaller it is true,[3] but closely
resembling those of Solomon, for they have wheeled
stands[4] and are decorated with cherubim (griffins),
vegetation and spirals (fig. XIII).

[1] In the *Bible du Centenaire*, 1,456 litres (320 gallons); according to
Father de Vaux, 'about 900 litres' (198 gallons), which is nevertheless
a considerable quantity and raises problems concerning their
mobility. See also Father Vincent's study, 'Les *mekôuôth*' in *Mélanges
B. Ubach* 1953.

[2] There are numerous reproductions: Benzinger, *Hebräische
Archäologie*, p. 219; H. Gressmann, *AOB*, Pl. CCIII; *Bible du Centenaire*,
II, p. 199.

[3] The wheeled laver from Larnaka is 39 cm. high and 23 cm. wide.

[4] At least in the Larnaka example.

Were these bowls intended to hold and carry the water needed for ablutions and lustrations (II Chron. 4.6), or were they symbolic cars representing years of heavy rainfall?[1]

Cult vessels. These include all the utensils required for the sacrificial rites, such as are found in all temples. They are briefly listed: pots, shovels, basins for sprinkling (I Kings 8.40, 45). They were all made by Hiram of 'polished bronze'.

*　　　　*　　　　*

This lavish use of metal is explained by the fact that Solomon had mines in the Araba[2] and foundries on the shores of the gulf of Aqaba, as Nelson Glueck's[3] excavations at Tell el Kheleifeh (Ezion-Geber)[4] have shown. But the bronze was cast on the banks of the Jordan (I Kings 7.46) with the assistance of Phoenician craftsmen under the direction of Hiram, who had clearly shown 'his skill, intelligence and knowledge' and made the best use of the resources of

[1] Suggested by A. Lods in the *Bible du Centenaire*, II, p. 199, who refers to bronze cauldrons mounted on wheels which were discovered in Europe at Pescatel in Mecklenburg and Milavec in Bohemia. Reproductions are given in Dechelette, *Manuel d'archéologie préhistorique*, II, pp. 285-6. It may be recalled that there were at one time 'sun chariots' in the Temple at Jerusalem on the evidence of II Kings 13.11.

[2] N. Glueck, 'King Solomon's Copper Mines', in *ILN*, July 7, 1934.

[3] *BASOR*, 79 (1940), pp. 2-18.

[4] This was also one of Solomon's important sea-ports (I Kings, 9.26), where gold from Ophir was disembarked; Ophir was probably on the west coast of Arabia, opposite Somaliland.

the country. In the Jordan valley conditions were ideal, for suitable earth was available for moulds, there was water in abundance and wind to operate the draught of his furnaces. No doubt the distance from Jerusalem caused transport difficulties, and it is not hard to imagine the terrific exertions required when the sea of bronze, for example, had to be conveyed to Jerusalem.

*   *   *

Ernest Renan was one of the first to point out that Solomon's Temple was 'a domestic Temple, a chapel of the palace',[1] and most modern scholars have supported this view,[2] for the building, including the walls, measured only 50 m. × 30 m. Nevertheless, this theory should not be pushed too far because the primary consideration should be the motive which actuated the building of the shrine. This was essentially to provide Yahweh with a *house*, in the literal sense of the word.[3] The Deity needed a home on earth, just as men did. The architectural plan of all Eastern temples, from the third millennium B.C., is based on that of an ordinary dwelling-house.[4]

[1] E. Renan, *Histoire du peuple d'Israël*, II (1891), p. 142.

[2] A. Lods, *La religion d'Israël*, p. 93: the Temple was primarily the chapel of the palace, like the one in the royal residence at Mari.

[3] *Bayith* in Hebrew, *bit* in Accadian.

[4] The Temples of Ishtar at Mari, Ninni-Zaza, for example.

In the course of time, however, the plan underwent modification. But even so the shrine was always a house[1]—that is to say, a dwelling-place. It was therefore primarily and essentially to provide a dwelling-place for Yahweh, who was present, as already mentioned, in the ark, that Solomon erected this building; its arrangement in three apartments (*ulâm, hekâl, debîr*) therefore dates from the tenth century B.C. This arrangement certainly had a symbolic significance, which has often exercised, and continues to exercise, the ingenuity of commentators.[2] It is possible that, as Josephus suggested, the three parts of the temple represented the three elements of the cosmos—water, earth and heaven—which corresponds, as has already been pointed out, to the biblical cosmogony (Ex. 20.4; Gen. 1.6).

The two bronze pillars, placed *in front* of the cosmos, might then represent those on which the earth, that is to say, the world rests.[3] According to tradition, the capitals of the pillars were richly decorated with pomegranates (I Kings 7.18-20), a fruit which, throughout the east, is the symbol of

[1] Another example from Mari may be cited: the Temple of Dagan dating from the second millennium, though not built on the plan of a dwelling, was still called a *house*, cf. G. Dossin, 'Inscriptions de fondation provenant de Mari', in *Syria*, XXI (1940), pp. 162-3.

[2] For a recent study on this subject see J. Daniélou, 'La symbolique cosmique du Temple de Jérusalem', in *Symbolisme cosmique et monuments religieux*, pp. 61-4. See also W. Vischer, *Les premiers prophètes*, pp. 365-6.

[3] Ps. 75.4; Job 9.6.

fertility, and for the religious sentiment of the time, Yahweh was the source of fruitfulness and prosperity.

It is obvious also that the decorative themes which appear on the panels of the doors and the woodwork of the *hekâl* are not merely ornamental. It has already been noted that cherubim, palm-trees, and roses[1] were common Syro-Phoenician and even Persian art-forms.[2] The whole design is certainly symbolic, and it may readily be admitted that its reproduction in the Temple of Jerusalem has an 'equivocal character'.[3] No doubt it could be explained as a reference to the garden of Eden and its guardian cherubim,[4] but a simpler explanation would be that Solomon had to allow a certain liberty to his foreign craftsmen who introduced their own ideas of decoration as well as their native architecture. It seems certain also that the number of golden candelabra—ten in all, five on the right (south) and five on the left (north)—has a symbolic significance. Benzinger, who regards the two bronze pillars as representing the sun and the moon, suggests that

[1] The word translated thus by Father de Vaux is rendered 'garlands of flowers' (*peture ṣiṣṣim*) by A. Lods in the *Bible du Centenaire*. Goodspeed and R.V., 'open flowers'. The term occurs nowhere else in the Old Testament.

[2] As may be seen from certain objects in the 'treasure of Ziwiye', which date from the ninth century B.C.

[3] W. Vischer, *op. cit.*, p. 369.

[4] *Ibid.*, p. 366, referring to Ezek. 28.13.

the candelabra represent the five other planets counted twice.[1] Since the identification of the pillars appears to be highly doubtful, the explanation is unsatisfactory. It would seem more probable that the number corresponds to one of the elements of Semitic arithmetic which was based on a decimal rather than the Sumerian sexagesimal system. It is possible that they were intended to recall the lights which illumined the earth (i.e. *hekâl*), but we are not told whether these lamps burned both day and night, as was to be the rule for the seven-branched lampstand in the second Temple. One would rather suppose that they were only lit at night, as had been the custom in the shrine at Shiloh (I Sam. 3.3), where there was one lamp only, which was extinguished at dawn.

The specific characteristics of the most holy place (*debîr*)—its cubic shape and the complete absence of lighting—are not easy to interpret. Its height was less than that of the *hekâl* (10 cubits instead of 15), which suggests that, besides having a lower ceiling, it was approached by a flight of steps. The *cella*—for this raised[2] chapel might be so described—contained no divine image, only the ark beneath its brooding cherubim, and this would not be visible

[1] I. Benzinger, *Hebräische Archäologie*, p. 330. In antiquity five planets were recognized: Saturn, Jupiter, Mars, Venus, Mercury; the sun and moon were added, making seven; one day was assigned to each.

[2] The *hekâl* constitutes the *antecella*.

[54]

unless the door of the *debîr* were open, which would not always be the case.[1]

Yahweh thus dwelt, and desired to dwell, in darkness.[2] This feature is characteristic, not of Mesopotamia, but of the temples of Egypt, in which, while the outer courts are open to the daylight, a series of colonnades, each more dimly lit than the last, leads to the inner shrine (*naos*), which is in complete darkness. In his prayer at the dedication of the Temple, Solomon seems to emphasize the contrast between Yahweh's creation of the sun— that is, of light—and his intention of remaining himself shrouded in darkness (I Kings 8.12),[3] but the reason is, and probably will always be, obscure.

*   *   *

Such was Solomon's Temple, the house built 'for the name' of Yahweh.[4] It remained almost intact until 586 B.C. It was, no doubt, a 'royal chapel', but it was also the heart and spiritual centre of the nation. Its situation close to other official or administrative buildings, as well as the part played by the king in the sacrificial cult,[5] demonstrate and emphasize the close connection between religion and the State. But this is not all: because of the existence of the Temple, God is actually present in

[1] I Kings 8.8.   [2] I Kings 8.12.

[3] W. Vischer, *Les premiers prophètes*, II, p. 366.

[4] The less vivid deuteronomic style. It is a fact, nonetheless, that throughout the East the 'name' is a reality and a presence.

[5] Solomon officiated as king and pontiff.

one particular place on earth and man can be
certain of finding him there. It is easy to understand
how the notion of this material presence at a point
in space later came to be regarded as an inadmissible
limitation imposed on the God of creation. 'Will
God indeed dwell in the earth? The heavens, even
the heaven of heavens, cannot contain thee; how
much less this house which I have built!' (I Kings
8.27).[1] Thus Solomon speaks when he is dedicating
to Yahweh the earthly habitation where 'his name'
at least will dwell (I Kings 8.29).

As the religious centre and spiritual home of the
nation, the Temple at Jerusalem was involved in all
the political events—internal and foreign—in the
history of the State, from the great days of Solomon
to its downfall in 586 B.C., through all the stages of
the great schism, the civil war between Israel and
Judah, the collapse of the kingdom of Samaria
(721 B.C.), the Assyrian menace at the time of
Sennacherib (701 B.C.), and the final destruction at
the hands of the Babylonians.

It is not surprising that the historical records
mention the Temple so frequently, for the most part
at moments of crisis. It was from the Temple

[1] According to Father de Vaux (*Les Livres des Rois*, p. 58, n. *a*)
this is 'a later insertion, which interrupts the narrative, and is
intended to avoid a materialistic interpretation of the divine presence
in the Temple' though it shows 'the lofty spiritual quality of the
religion of Israel'. This is certainly true of the time of the Deuter-
onomist, that is at the period of Josiah's reform in 621 B.C.

treasure that the kings raised the heavy tribute of gold and silver demanded by ruthless conquerors or by foreign kings whose support was sought: Asa of Judah (911-870) by this means secured an alliance with Ben-hadad of Damascus (I Kings 15.18); Jehoash of Judah (II Kings 12.18); Jehoash of Israel (798-783) plundered it after his victory over Amaziah (II Kings 14.14); as already mentioned, Ahaz (736-716) used it to propitiate the Assyrian king Tiglathpileser (II Kings, 16.8), and went so far as to change the ritual furnishings of the outer court in deference to that monarch (II Kings 16.17); Hezekiah himself had to draw on it (II Kings 18.15) to appease Sennacherib (701 B.C.).

It was in the Temple also that the high-priest Jehoiadah concealed the young prince Joash, whom he had rescued from the diabolical frenzy of Athaliah (II Kings 11.3). When the child was grown up, the high-priest caused him to appear with all due ceremony at the door of the Temple—that is, in front of the portico. After the proclamation and the anointing, the new king, having been acclaimed, 'stood by the pillar' (II Kings 11.14)—that is, one of the two bronze pillars already described (p. 26). This was undoubtedly the position decreed by law and custom, for it is mentioned again in connection with Josiah (640-609) the reformer, when he went up to the Temple and renewed the covenant with Yahweh (II Kings 23.3).

It was a solemn moment. Ungodly kings had introduced pagan cults in Jerusalem. Manasseh (687-642 B.C.) in particular had 'built altars even in the house of Yahweh' (II Kings 21.4-5). So Josiah, relying on the support of Jeremiah, determined to sweep away all these abominations. Taking advantage of the discovery of the 'Book of the Law', which had come to light when the restoration and repair of the Temple were being carried out,[1] he was even more active than his predecessor Hezekiah[2] (716-687 B.C.) and embarked on a thoroughgoing and ruthless clearance. According to the biblical records, he turned out 'all the [cultic] vessels which had been made for Baal, for Asherah[3] and for all the hosts of heaven' (II Kings 23.4), 'the horses which the kings of Judah had dedicated to the sun[4] at the doorway of the Temple' and 'he burned the chariot of the sun' (v. 11). There were also altars which were placed 'on the roof' (v. 12)[5] on which sacrifices were

[1] They are mentioned several times: II Kings 12.7, 12-14, 22.5-6.

[2] II Kings 18.4.

[3] The goddess Asherah was worshipped in the form of a pole. We are told that the king had it burned in the valley of Kidron (II Kings 23.6). See a recent study on Asherah by W. L. Reed, *The Asherah in the Old Testament* (1949).

[4] Among the Assyrians the sun god Shamash was represented standing on a horse; cf. the reliefs of Maltaia.

[5] Cuneiform ritual texts provide evidence of rites celebrated on the roofs of temples in Babylon. See Thureau-Dangin, *Rituels accadiens*, pp. 122-3. One of these texts is reproduced in the author's *Ziggurats et Tour de Babel*, p. 119.

undoubtedly offered to propitiate the gods; and those altars built by Manasseh 'in the two courts of the house of Yahweh' (v. 12)[1] which were pulled down and cast out. Such was the extent of the desecration which had developed from Solomon's action, when, to please the women of his harem, he set up high places in the immediate neighbourhood of Jerusalem (I Kings 11.5-8). The process went on without hindrance, and was even accelerated when Manasseh and Amon, eager to propitiate Assyria, allowed the Temple itself to be polluted.

Nevertheless, in spite of the firm stand made by Josiah, the days of the Temple were numbered. On one occasion already, in 701 B.C., the end had seemed to be imminent. Hezekiah, in the Temple itself, had called upon Yahweh to take notice of the threats of Assyria (II Kings 19.14 *et seq.*), but the prophet Isaiah had promised that it should be saved, and so it was.

But the miracle was not repeated. The hour of its destruction arrived, this time at the hands of Nebuchadnezzar's Babylonians (604-562 B.C.). It was effected in two stages: the beleaguered city was taken (597 B.C.); part of the population, including the prophet Ezekiel, was carried away into captivity. Jerusalem was sacked and the Temple was looted (II Kings 24.13). Eleven years later, when the

[1] It is not possible to identify, from archaeological evidence, this architectural notation, at any rate with reference to Solomon's Temple.

new king Zedekiah rose in rebellion, the king of Babylon returned to complete the work of destruction. The city defended itself vigorously for a year and a half, but finally had to surrender. This time the Babylonians ravaged, pillaged, and burned it. The 'Chaldeans broke up the bronze pillars of the house of Yahweh, and the stands [of the bowls] and the sea of bronze which were in the house of Yahweh, and they carried away the bronze to Babylon' (II Kings 25.13). They also took all the vessels and ritual objects. The Temple of Solomon was no more.

II

THE TEMPLE OF EZEKIEL

This is not the place to discuss at length the shrine known by the name of the prophet Ezekiel. It was the subject of a vision and never actually built. However, the general plan may be briefly indicated because of its influence, and that of the theological concept which it represented, on the architecture of the temple built by Herod more than five hundred years later.

In 572-571, twenty-five years after his departure into exile, the prophet had a vision of Israel restored and the Temple raised again from its ruins (Ezek. 40-44). The emphasis is chiefly on the idea of ritual holiness. In the Jerusalem of Solomon's time, as has been pointed out, the Temple and the Palace were situated so close to one another that the Temple was to all appearance a royal chapel. But Ezekiel's Temple is a whole in itself, strictly separated and isolated, not only from the palace but from the whole city.

The exact extent and the measurements of the area of the first Temple are not known, but no such

[61]

doubt exists with regard to Ezekiel's Temple. The enclosure was in the form of a great square (fig. XIV), the sides measuring 500 cubits (250 m.)

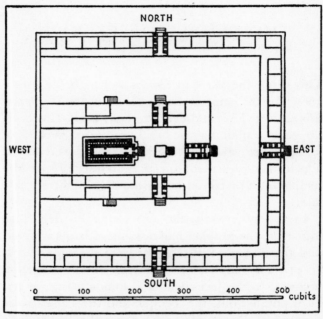

XIV. Ezekiel's Temple (from Benzinger, op. cit.)

(Ezek. 42.16-20). It had three gateways, placed on the east, north, and south. These gave access to the first, or outer, court, which enclosed another, also entered by three gateways similarly placed, each in line with one of the gateways of the outer court.

These gates, moreover, were of the type known as 'fortified' (i.e. with guardrooms on either side), examples of which have been found on a number of sites;[1] they are described with a wealth of detail

XV. (a) The Altar of Ezekiel's Temple
(b) Altar of Meziddo

(Ezek. 40.6-16) and clearly indicate how strictly the right of entry was to be controlled. Indeed no stranger, no uncircumcised person, could gain access to the shrine (44.9) and only the priests could officiate, that is, could enter the inner court and approach the altar and the sanctuary.

Every detail of the altar is precisely described (43.13-17). It was in the form of a ziggurat (fig. XV) or a tower of several stories. Set on a base 18 cubits (9 m.) square, it reached a height of 11

[1] The gateways of Shechem and Beth-Shemesh in Palestine; the gate of Carchemish in the Hittite country. Diagrams are given in Kurt Galling's *Biblisches Reallexikon*, under *Tor*, cols. 523-4.

cubits and four horns[1] were placed at the angles of the upper surface.[2] This characteristic design so closely resembles the relief in the Louvre which shows a *ziggurat* ornamented with horns[3] that it would be difficult to deny the relationship between the altar of Ezekiel's vision and the Mesopotamian *ziggurat*.[4]

The sanctuary, like Solomon's, consisted of three chambers. A detailed description, with measurements, is given (40.48-41.1-26) and the same terminology is used—*ulâm* (porch or portico), *hekâl* (holy place)—for the first two sections; the third is explicitly described as 'the holy of holies' (41.4).

The building was 100 cubits (50 m.) long[5] and was raised on a platform approached by a stairway

[1] A number of stone altars have been found in Palestine and Phoenicia with the top adorned with horns. For instances in the Bible see Ex. 27.2, 28.2; I Kings 1.50.

[2] The upper surface is called *har'el*, a word which Albright derives from the Accadian *arallu*=underworld or mountain of the gods (*ARI*, p. 151). Strangely enough, the base of the altar is called (Ezek. 43.14) *heq ha'arês*=the bosom of the earth, a term which recalls the Babylonian phrase *irat ersiti* (bosom of the earth) used by Nebuchadnezzar to describe the foundations of the *ziggurat* of Babylon. See also Vincent, in *Analecta Bollandiana*, LXVII (1949), pp. 7-20, and the reconstruction of this altar by Stevens in *BA*, XVIII (1955), p. 43.

[3] A relief from Nineveh; a drawing of it is given in the author's *The Tower of Babel*, Studies in Biblical Archaeology, No. 2, p. 29. A number of altars with horns have been reported from Phoenician and Palestinian sites, cf. Fig. XV.

[4] *The Tower of Babel*, p. 34.

[5] The first Temple was 60 cubits (50 m.) long (I Kings, 6.2). Herod's Temple was to be 100.

3. The exterior precincts of the Haram esh-Sherif, from the South-east

4. South-east angle of the precincts of the Haram. Site of the 'pinnacle' of the Temple

of ten steps[1] flanked by 'pillars'[2] (Ezek. 40.49). The portico measured 20 × 12 cubits, the *hekál* 40 × 20 cubits, the holy of holies 20 × 20 cubits.

All the walls were panelled and decorated with carved cherubim and palm-trees[3] (fig. XVI), as

XVI. Cherubim on either side of a palmetto (from Arslan Tash, p. 131)

were the panels of the doors and the breastwork of the vestibules. There is one detail which defies illustration, that is a cherub with two faces, a human face turned towards the palm-tree on one side, and a lion's face turned towards the palm-tree on the other side (Ezek. 41.18-19). There are no monuments which might provide a comparison.[4]

[1] This information is taken as evidence for the stairway which is assumed to have existed in Solomon's Temple.

[2] These are undoubtedly the pillars Jachin and Boaz.

[3] 'A palm-tree between two cherubim' is the description given in Ezek. 41.18. This is the characteristic oriental and Mesopotamian motif of animals placed one on either side of a palm-tree or palmetto; there are numerous examples.

[4] Deities with two faces (prototypes of the Roman Janus) or even with four are found in the iconography of Mesopotamia, see H. Frankfort, 'More Sculpture from the Diyala Region' (*OIP*, LX), Pl. 77, 78, but nothing corresponding to the cherubim.

Surprisingly enough, very little is said about the equipment and the ritual vessels. There is an altar of wood in the *hekâl* (41.2-22), a reproduction of the 'table of shewbread' of the first Temple. There is no mention of lights, no suggestion of the richness and the magnificence of Solomon's Temple, with its woodwork, doors and even its floor overlaid with gold. Not a word about the ark: the ancient palladium had vanished, but there was no longer any need for it to proclaim the presence of Yahweh in the midst of his people. For the 'glory of the God of Israel' had returned from the east with a sound like the sound of many waters and filled the whole Temple (43.1-5).

Since the whole area within the enclosure has become 'most holy ground' (43.12), the cleavage between priests and laity, pure and impure, is absolute. Nothing unclean, nothing secular may come in contact with the holy God. For this reason, within the enclosure itself there are two zones, to provide for the co-existence of two separate worlds. Hence the importance assigned to the 'buildings' attached to the sanctuary. Not only is the Temple itself surrounded by three stories of side chambers,[1] but there is a series of rooms in each of the two courts and even kitchens (46.19-24).[2] There is no need for

[1] As in Solomon's sanctuary.

[2] A. Lods, 'Les cuisines du Temple de Jérusalem', in *RHR*, CXXVII (1944), pp. 30-54.

further discussion on the situation of these buildings, since they never actually existed.[1]

The vision concludes with a superb symbol. From the new Temple a spring of living water, gushing like a torrent, would flow by the valley of Kidron to the Dead Sea, the waters of which would become sweet, and that desolate region would blossom like Paradise, its trees always in leaf and bearing fruit each month of the year (Ezek. 47.1-12). Such was the picture of the future which the prophet of the exile, carried away in ecstasy 'beside the River Khebar',[2] presented to his people. His hopes were no less sublime than his vision. When the time for action came, Ezekiel was most probably dead, 'not having received the promises but only having seen them and greeted them from afar'.[3] Others were to take in hand the rebuilding of the ruins, but the means were not adequate to the requirements. The great design could not be carried out, and more modest plans had to be adopted.[4]

[1] In Herod's Temple one room was set apart for the making of the bread for the table of shewbread. For the annexes to the Temple (Ezek. 42.1 *et seq.*) see K. Elliger 'Die grossen Tempel-sakristeien in Verfassungsentwurf des Ezechiels,' in *Geschichte und Altes Testament* (Festschrift Alt) pp. 79-103.

[2] The Babylonian *naru kabaru*, tributary of the Euphrates, not far from the ancient Sumerian city of Nippur, to the south of Babylon.

[3] Heb. 11.13.

[4] In the Aramaean fragments of Qumran 2 there is a description with measurements of the Temple in terms which recall Ezekiel (see *RB*, 1955, pp. 22-245).

III

THE SECOND TEMPLE

After the collapse of the Babylonian power and the capture of Babylon by Cyrus in 539 B.C., the whole of the Near East experienced a real deliverance. The policy of the new conqueror was indeed very different from that which had dictated the actions of the Assyrians or the Neo-Babylonians. Though he was an autocratic sovereign, his authority was tinctured with clemency and generosity. The conquered peoples, who had been rigidly governed by satraps, themselves closely controlled, were in future to preserve (or to regain) their own laws, their religion, their languages and, in many cases, their own kings. From one or other of his palaces—Susa, Persepolis, Ecbatana—the 'king of kings' controlled, directed, promulgated his requirements. It is easy to understand the enthusiasm and the joy with which certain visionaries greeted the change: Cyrus must be the anointed one of Yahweh (Isa. 45.1) who had directly inspired him to rebuild his city and set his exiles free (v. 13).

In 538 the decree was signed, permitting all those

who so desired to return to Palestine.[1] Not all the
exiles took advantage of it, for many of them had
succeeded in making good positions for themselves[2]
in Babylon, which they had no desire to abandon in
order to return to the barren and unrewarding land
of their ancestors. The first party left Mesopotamia
in 537 B.C.,[3] Zerubbabel and Jeshua being among
their leaders. Cyrus had given back to them the
vessels, numbering several thousand,[4] which Nebuchadnezzar had taken from the Temple of Yahweh.
This generous gesture also was in keeping with
the character of Cyrus, for there is evidence from
cuneiform documents that he restored to several
Mesopotamian shrines the statues of gods which
Nabonides, king of Babylon, had stolen and set up
in his capital.[5] Cyrus could not restore to the Jews

[1] Dhorme, 'Cyrus le Grand', in *RB*, 1912, pp. 22-49; Father de
Vaux, 'Les décrets de Cyrus et de Darius sur la reconstruction du
Temple', in *RB*, 1937, pp. 29-57. The text of the decree is given twice,
in Ezra 1.2-4. and 6.2-5, with a short summary in II Chron. 36.23.
Recent French studies on these matters have been written by A.
Gelin, *Esdras-Néhémie*, and Frank Michaeli, 'Le Temple et la Loi', a
thesis for a Doctorate in Theology, unpublished.

[2] The archives of Nippur mention Jewish bankers practising their
profession in that city at the time of Artaxerxes I (465-424 B.C.).
The most recent study on the subject is that of G. Cardascia, *Les
Archives des Murashû, une famille d'hommes d'affaires babyloniens à l'epoque
perse* (455-403 B.C.), Paris, 1951.

[3] According to Ezra 2.64, 42,360 people, in addition to 7,327
slaves and 200 choristers.

[4] The figure varies in the different texts from 2,499 to 5,499. See
Bible du Centenaire, note to Ezra 1-9; R.V. gives 5,400.

[5] The most important of these texts is the Rassam Cylinder in the
British Museum, *RB*, 1937, p. 31.

the statue of Yahweh, since none existed, and the ark was certainly not among the spoil captured by Nebuchadnezzar; he could only give them what remained from the pillage of 586—that is to say, the gold and silver vessels of their cult (Ezra 1.9).

It is not altogether clear what the exiles did and how they comported themselves after their return to Palestine. It seems that, in the face of the considerable difficulties they encountered, they contented themselves at first with restoring the altar (Ezra. 3.3-4) so that they could offer sacrifices to Yahweh. In addition they attacked the task of clearing or putting into some sort of order the chaotic mass of ruins.[1]

Eighteen years passed, concerning which there is practically no information. The Jews were only a small group, and they had to defend themselves against hostility on every side. At last, in the second year of the reign of Darius I (522-485), thanks to the driving power of two forceful personalities, Jeshua and Zerubbabel, and with the support of the prophets Haggai and Zechariah, they set to work to rebuild the Temple (Ezra 5.1-2; Hag. 1.14-19). These activities aroused the suspicions of the governor of the Fifth or Transeuphratean satrapy, a certain Tattenai, who reported them to his master Darius. He, however, observing the edict of Cyrus, gave permission for the work to proceed

[1] The Books of Ezra and Haggai are the chief sources on this point.

(Ezra. 6.6-12).[1] Building went on for five years and was completed therefore in 515 B.C.[2]

Little is known about this Temple. Most probably it followed the plan of Solomon's sanctuary, using similar materials and techniques: large stones with timber joists in the walls (Ezra 5.8). The dimensions are recorded: length 60 cubits (30 m.), height 60 cubits[3] (Ezra 6.3). Though the main plan might have been the same as Solomon's, it is certain that the magnificence of the first Temple was not reproduced. Those few survivors who could remember the time before the exile and draw comparisons did not conceal their disappointment;[4] but how was it possible to do better, for the golden age of Solomon had passed away? In spite of the help of the kindly Achaemenian king (Ezra 6.8), it was clearly impossible to incur expenditure on the scale of those days when, as the Book of Kings has it, 'silver was common as stone in Jerusalem' (I Kings 10.27).

[1] This would seem to be the only way to reconcile two apparently contradictory statements, according to which the work of rebuilding began either in the second year (Ezra 3.8-13) or not till eighteen years after the return from exile (Hag. 1.14-15); the 'second year of Darius' was 520 B.C.

[2] Ezra 6.15, the 'twelfth month of the sixth year of the reign of Darius'.

[3] The text here is defective. The width is not given, and one would have expected the height to be the same as Solomon's Temple, 30 cubits (not 60). See *Bible du Centenaire*, n. to Ezra 6.3.

[4] Ezra 3.12-13; Haggai 2.3. According to Josephus, the Temple area measured 154 m. by 52 m. 50 cm. This is very different from the dimensions of Ezekiel's vision.

Nor were the furnishings[1] so rich or costly. The 'holy of holies' was empty, for the lost ark had not been replaced. A single slab of stone marked its place. Each year, on the Day of Atonement, the

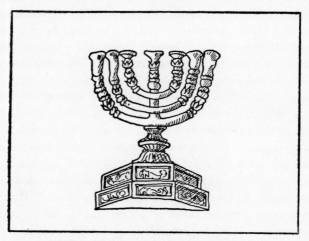

XVII. The Seven-Branched Lampstand

high-priest placed his censer on it.[2] In the *hekâl* stood the golden altar of incense, the table for the shewbread, and a seven-branched lampstand (fig. XVII) in place of the ten candelabra of Solomon's day. It is not known where, if anywhere,

---

[1] For the furnishings, see various notices in I Mac. 1.21, 4.49-51.

[2] Josephus, *The Jewish War*, V, 5, 5; Mishna, *Yoma*, 5, 2, according to which the stone slab was called *eben shetijjâ*.

in the new building, the decoration described in Ezekiel's vision was placed.

It seems unlikely that the strict regulations adumbrated by Ezekiel were enforced. It is certain, however, that there were two courts, an outer one to which everyone was admitted, and an inner court which only Jews in a condition of Levitical purity might enter. The existence of this regulation has been shown by E. Bikermann in his commentary on a decree of Antiochus III of Syria (223-187 B.C.), previously mistranslated and misinterpreted.[1]

Indirect confirmation is provided by the well-known incident which occurred when the Jewish king Alexander Jannaeus (103-76 B.C.) entered the Temple on one of the days of the Feast of Tabernacles[2] and was pelted with citrons by a crowd of resentful worshippers who had found their way into the inner court where the altar stood.

It is also established that the adjoining buildings (side rooms) were situated in one or other of these courts. According to Nehemiah (13.4-9), a stranger, the Ammonite Tobiah, was occupying one of the rooms set apart for the vessels, the offerings, and the incense used in the cult. He was, however, ejected.

The second Temple was also destined to be

[1] E. Bikerman, 'Une proclamation séleucide relative au Temple de Jérusalem', in *Syria*, XXV (1946-8), pp. 67-85. There are a number of references in Maccabees to these different courts, but they are not very explicit: I Mac. 4.38, 48; 7.33; 9.54; II Mac. 6.4.

[2] Josephus, *Jewish Antiquities*, XIII, 13, 5; *Jewish War*, I, 4, 3.

plundered and finally profaned. In 168 B.C. the
Seleucid king Antiochus Epiphanes occupied Jerusalem, entered the Temple, and removed the seven-
branched lampstand, the golden altar, and all the
costly vessels. A year later, on December 15, 167,
he profaned the Temple of Yahweh by setting up in
it 'the abomination of desolation'.[1] Once again the
sacrificial ritual came to an end.

It was restored three years afterwards when the
victorious insurgents reoccupied Jerusalem and
'purified' the Temple.[2] The pagan altar was
destroyed, and the former altar of burnt offerings,
which had been defiled, was also demolished. A new
one was made, of unhewn stone according to the
Law. The sanctuary was restored and refurnished
with a seven-branched lampstand, an altar of incense
and a table for the shewbread.[3] The façade of the
Temple was decorated with gold crowns and shields;
all the auxiliary buildings were reconstructed. On
December 25, 164,[4] the Feast of the Dedication
of the purified Temple was celebrated, and the

[1] I Mac. 1.54. Cf. Dan. 9.27; Mark, 13.14. It was a statue either
of Olympian Jupiter or of Baal-Shamin (*RB*, 1930, pp. 188-9), or
possibly a pagan altar placed on the Jewish altar (L. Randon, *Les
livres apocryphes de l'Ancien Testament*, p. 14, n. *g*).

[2] I Mac. 4.36-59.

[3] I Mac. 4.49 adds an 'altar of burnt offerings', but this was in the
court and therefore outside, not within, the sanctuary.

[4] G. Ricciotti, *Histoire d'Israël*, II, p. 311; Abel, *Histoire de la
Palestine*, I, p. 142.

occasion was commemorated every year afterwards (John 10.22).[1]

A hundred years later the Romans entered Jerusalem. By that time the Temple, defended by strong ramparts,[2] had become a veritable citadel. Pompey's troops besieged it for three months before they were able to effect an entry early in the autumn of 63 B.C. The priests who were offering sacrifices were slaughtered at the altar. Pompey entered the Temple and approached the holy of holies, but, out of respect for the religion of the defeated people, he touched nothing—not even treasure worth two thousand talents—and left everything in its place. But the fact that even one pagan had set his unclean feet in the holy place constituted, for pious Jews, an indelible pollution. Nevertheless, the practice of the cult was revived and sacrifices were once more offered. No one could have foreseen that the end of the second Temple was at hand and that a king would give his name to a grandiose reconstruction inspired by ambition rather than religious feeling.

[1] The feast was called the *Hanukkah* in the Jewish liturgical calendar. Reference may be made to two recent studies on the Feast of Tabernacles: Father Abel, in *RB*, 1946, pp. 538-46, and R. J. Zwi Werblowsky, in *RHR*, CXLV, 1 (1954), pp. 30-68.

[2] Built by the Maccabees, I Mac. 4.60.

IV

HEROD'S TEMPLE

After the taking of Jerusalem by Pompey (63 B.C.), Palestine came under the direct control of Rome and was administered by the Procurator of Syria. The task of administration was not an easy one, for there were constant risings to be suppressed as well as internal strife between the descendants of the Maccabees—the Hasmonaeans—and the astute and cunning Idumeans. Relations between Edom and Judah had always been bad, for bitter hatred divided the two countries.[1] When therefore Herod, son of the Idumean Antipater, succeeded in getting himself recognized as king of Jerusalem and Palestine, the event was anything but welcome to the nation. Confronted by mistrust, if not actual hostility, the new king endeavoured to conciliate his resentful subjects by pursuing a policy of magnificence designed to enhance his own prestige and to produce in the people the illusion of national independence. But Herod was too intelligent not to be aware that his

[1] This is evident from the following references: Ps. 137.7-9; Ezek. 35.5, 10-12, 15; Obad. 10-16.

[76]

practice of adopting Western customs[1] would gain him little sympathy, and that to win favour with the people he would have to embark on some spectacular project. Nothing seemed to offer a more profitable opportunity than the total rebuilding of the 'house of Yahweh', more particularly since the Temple which had been erected after the return from exile had neither the grandeur nor the magnificence of Solomon's Temple. Moreover, the passage of five centuries had left on it marks of age and decay.

Having made the decision, Herod exerted himself to the utmost to avoid wounding the susceptibilities of the rigorists. After engaging ten thousand workmen, he had a thousand priests trained as stonemasons to work in the most holy parts of the sanctuary. Moreover, in planning the architecture, he was careful not to include any detail in the structure or the decoration which might offend traditional religious sentiment.[2] His primary purpose was to enlarge and beautify the Temple so that it should be worthy, not so much of the God to whom it was consecrated as of the dignity of the king whose achievement it was. Herod, although he found his inspiration in Greek culture, was nevertheless a

[1] He had built, or was about to build, in Jerusalem a number of typically Roman edifices: a theatre, a circus, a hippodrome, not to mention the modernization of Samaria, which was rebuilt in most magnificent style, with a temple dedicated to Augustus!

[2] It was not till later that a golden eagle was placed on the front of the porch of the Temple, and it was removed as the result of popular agitation not long before the king's death.

Semite and as such respected two of the fundamental principles of the Jewish cult: the Temple was the house of Yahweh and in its precincts Yahweh met his people who had come to offer sacrifices to him. This was the reason why so much thought was given to the arrangement of the holy house, and why such care was taken to provide space enough for the faithful to assemble in the meeting-place.

*   *   *

The great undertaking was begun in the eighteenth year of Herod's reign, 20-19 B.C. Although the essential structure was completed in ten years (9 B.C.), work went on, with various interruptions, until A.D. 64. This explains the words said to Jesus: 'Forty and six years[1] was this Temple in building, and wilt thou raise it up in three days?' (John 2.20).

The building was enormous, the largest of all Herod's architectural achievements. According to Josephus, who, apart from the Mishna, is the chief source of information, its area was almost twice that of the court of the earlier Temple. This was effected by cutting into the rock of the hill on the Bezetha side and, a more difficult operation, adding to it on the south[2] by building up an embankment

---

[1] These words must have been spoken in A.D. 27; their importance for fixing the date of the ministry of Jesus is obvious.

[2] For the architecture of Herod's Temple see C. Watzinger, *Denkmäler Palästinas*, II, pp. 34-6; G. Dalman, *Les itinéraires de Jésus*, pp. 370-401. Although written ninety years ago, de Vogüés' book, *Le Temple de Jérusalem*, is still valuable, but the definitive study will

reinforced by thick walls, thus providing the platform. Some idea of the magnitude of the operation may be gained from the following figures: it has been established, from measurements carried out by Warren in 1867-8, that at the south-east angle (fig. XVIII) there was a difference of 47 m. between the

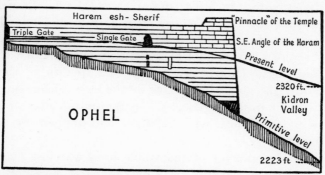

XVIII. South-eastern angle of the Haram (from Vincent, Jérusalem antique, *Pl. II, 2)*

rock on which the foundation was laid and the level of the inner court. At the south-west angle the difference is less, but even so amounts to 30 m.[1] In the same sector twenty-five courses of stone-work

certainly be Volume II of Father Vincent's *Jérusalem de l'Ancien Testament*, Paris, 1956. A paper by the same author, 'Le temple hérodien d'après la Mishnah' in *RB*, 1954, pp. 5-53 (to be continued) is a very important critical examination of the treatise *Middoth* in relation to the Temple.

[1] Watzinger, *op. cit.*, p. 34, from which the data which follow are taken. According to Abel, *Histoire de la Palestine*, I, p. 373, the south-eastern angle was 41 metres high.

are still extant, fourteen of which may be seen on the external surface of what is known as 'the wailing wall' (Pl. 5).

The Herodian style of building may be easily recognized by the thickness and size of the blocks. The average height is 1 m. 20 cm. to 1 m. 2 cm., sometimes more (1 m. 85 cm. to 1 m. 75 cm.), and some are as long as 9 to 12 metres. It is easy to understand the admiring exclamations of the disciples: 'Master, behold, what manner of stones and what manner of buildings!' (Mark 13.1). And the quality of the cutting is equally impressive, for the surface is smooth, without projecting bosses. On the outside the wall was heightened with pilasters and topped by a cornice.[1]

The perimeter of the whole area was just over 1,380 metres. It was trapezoid in shape, measuring 480 metres on the west and 300 metres on the north.[2] It was entered by eight gates: two on the south, four on the west, one on the north and one on the east.

The two gateways (fig. XIX) on the south side are called in the Mishna 'the doors of Huldah'; their main structure dates from the time of Herod, as does the inner vestibule with its pilasters and columns into

[1] The best example, still visible today, is that provided by the Haram of Hebron; see Vincent, Mackay and Abel, *Le Haram el Khalil*, Pl. III.

[2] The present dimensions of the Haram esh-Sherif are: west, 491 m.; east, 462 m.; north, 310 m.; south, 281 m. The dimensions of the Temple of Jupiter at Damascus are 315 m. × 270 m.; those of the Acropolis of Athens are 240 m. × 120 m.

5. The 'Wailing Wall'. Foundations of Herod's Temple

6. General view of the Mosque of the Rock

7. The Mosque of the Rock from the South

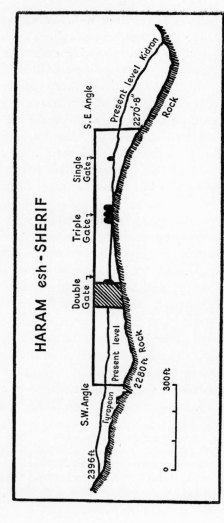

XIX. *South Front of the Haram (from Warren, Recovery, 119)*

which they open: this vestibule today is beneath the Mosque el Aqsa. The 'triple doorway' is a Byzantine reconstruction of an earlier 'double doorway' connected with the arrangement of the so-called 'stables of Solomon' close by. These two southern gates originally measured 12 m. 50 cm. and 11 m. 90 cm. respectively.[1] Covered passage-ways, made under the royal portico, led up to the court of the Gentiles.[2] Another gate, not far from the south-eastern angle, and described as 'single' (Pl. 5), was really a postern and nothing remains of it but a pointed arch and a hole in the wall.

There were four gates on the western side—that is, facing towards the new city. The first, known as 'Barclay's', was rather more than 82 metres from the south-west angle, and its dimensions were 5 m. 50 cm. wide and 8 m. 75 cm. high, with a massive lintel 7 m. 50 cm. $\times$ 2 m. 8 cm.[3] The largest of the three others was probably that known as the 'Coponius Gate,'[4] situated at the junction of the two main roads which ran east to west and north to south through Jerusalem. From this side, the only means of communication between the Temple and the city were by viaducts spanning the Tyropœon valley, parts of

[1] Watzinger, *op. cit.*, II, p. 39. There is a reproduction of these gates in de Vogüé, *Le Temple de Jérusalem*, Pls. IV and VI.

[2] It could truthfully be said of those who went into the sanctuary by this way that they went *up* to the Temple. Cf. Luke, 18.10.

[3] Watzinger, *op. cit.*, II, p. 38. This is de Vogüé's 'western gate'.

[4] Now on the site of Bab es-Silsile (the Gate of the Chain).

which have been discovered (Wilson's arch and Robinson's arch).[1]

On the north side, the side of Bezetha, there was only one gate, called 'Tadi' and, according to the Mishna, never used.

Finally, on the east side, in the direction of Kidron and opposite the Mount of Olives, there was one gate, now called the Susa Gate; today this is on the site of the Golden Gate, and in its present condition probably dates from the early days of Islam. It is approximately the same width as the gates on the south side and its threshold is on the same level; it seems likely, therefore, that the substructure dates from the time of Herod.[2]

Thus there is reason to believe that it was by this gate that Jesus, coming from Bethphage, entered the Temple on Palm Sunday (Mark 11.11; Matt. 21.12; Luke 19.45). This was also the most direct route from the Temple to Bethany (Mark 11.11).

The whole area within the walls was divided into two separate but concentric courts:[3] the first, or outer, court was that of the Gentiles; the second, lying within it, was itself divided into sections

[1] Vincent, *Jérusalem de l'Ancien Testament*, I, pp. 58-64, Pls. XVIII, XIX. Robinson's arch was in the continuation of the central aisle of the 'royal porch'.

[2] Watzinger, *op. cit.*, II, p. 41.

[3] A typically Semitic design, according to which there might be either a succession of courts (Baalbek) or courts within courts (Palmyra, Temple of Bel).

reserved respectively for women, for men, for the priests and, finally, for God himself (fig. XX).

The court of the Gentiles was surrounded on four sides by 'porches'.[1] On the south was the 'royal porch', consisting of three aisles and four rows of pillars, the last being attached to the wall. Its total width was more than 32 metres and there were one hundred and sixty-two pillars[2] supporting a wooden ceiling richly carved. The girth of each pillar was so great that three men could scarcely encircle it.[3] The central aisle was one and a half times as wide and twice as high as the two side aisles.

What was this porch used for? It is possible that the merchants and the money-changers carried on their business there;[4] hence the well-known incident of Jesus expelling 'the merchants from the Temple' (John 2.14-16; Matt. 21.12-13; Mark 11.15; Luke 21.45-6).

On the east, north and south sides the porches had two rows of pillars; they were 30 cubits (15 m.) wide and formed covered galleries, roofed but opening on to the court. Each pillar consisted of a plain stone shaft 25 cubits in height (12 m. 50 cm.)

---

[1] The only description of these is to be found in Josephus, *Antiquities* XV, 410-16. Here also see Watzinger, *op. cit.*, II, pp. 39-40.

[2] The figures given by Josephus are often inaccurate; thus he mentions a perimeter of 6 stadia and a length of 1 stadium (185 m.) for this porch, which measured 280 m.

[3] The diameter may therefore be estimated at about 1 m. 60 cm.

[4] Dalman, *op. cit.*, p. 383.

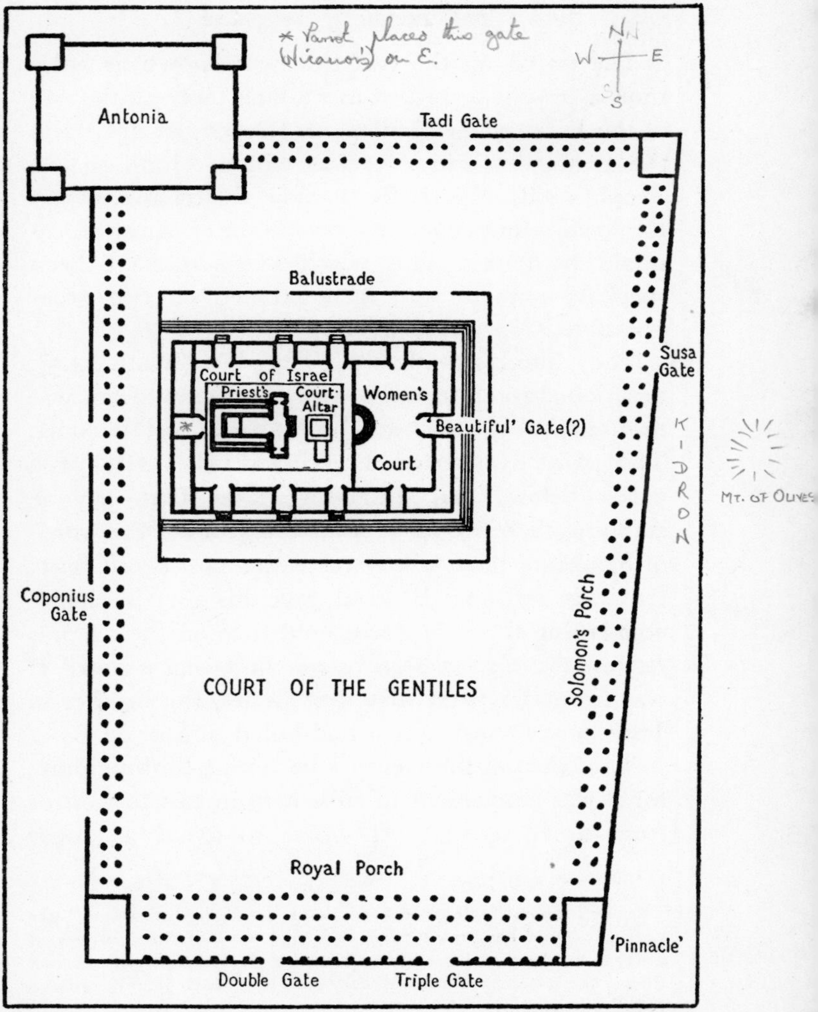
Antonia
Tadi Gate
Balustrade
Court of Israel
Priest's Court
Altar
Women's
Court
'Beautiful' Gate(?)
Susa Gate
Coponius Gate
COURT OF THE GENTILES
Solomon's Porch
Royal Porch
'Pinnacle'
Double Gate
Triple Gate
KIDRON
MT. OF OLIVES
* Parrot places this gate (Nicanor's) on E.
N
W
E
S

XX. The Temple of Herod. Plan of the General Structure
(*from* Dictionnaire encyclopédique de la Bible)

The porch on the east side was known as Solomon's. Jesus is described as walking there on the day of the Feast of the Dedication (December 25),[1] and the Evangelist adds: 'It was winter' (John 10.22). People used, apparently, to take shelter there from the cold while enjoying such winter sunshine as might be found. This porch seems to have been specially popular and is mentioned on two other occasions: Acts 3.11, 5.12.[2]

The 'pinnacle of the Temple' (Matt. 4.5), mentioned in connection with the Temptation, was most probably at the south-east angle of this court. This point overlooked the Kidron valley some 100 yards below, and Josephus states that anyone standing there would become dizzy. Thus the words of Satan are particularly relevant: *'Cast thyself down, for it is written: He will give his angels charge concerning thee, they will hold thee on their hands for fear that thy foot shall be crushed against a stone.'* It was from this place also that James, the brother of Jesus, was thrown down and killed in A.D. 62.

The court of the Gentiles became a thoroughfare, for it was convenient to cross it from east to west or from north to south in order to avoid a longer

---

[1] See above, p. 5.

[2] The incident of Jesus in the Temple at the age of twelve (Luke 2.41-50) would have taken place in one or other of these porches, as also the teaching and the discussions with the Pharisees and Scribes during the last days of the ministry of Jesus (Mark 11.27-12.40 and parallel passages).

journey round it. It had thus taken on the character of a public highway, and this explains why Jesus would not permit 'any man to go through the Temple carrying a load' (Mark 11.16).

*   *   *

Within the court of the Gentiles, but not exactly in the centre, stood the Temple proper, set on a small terrace surrounded by a stone balustrade about 1 m. 50 cm. in height, on which were placed, at intervals, inscriptions in Latin and Greek prohibiting strangers from passing through the barrier. Two examples of the Greek text are extant[1] and run thus:

'Strangers are forbidden to pass the barrier and enter the precincts of the sanctuary. Anyone found doing so will himself be responsible for the death penalty which will be inflicted on him.'

This text has been interpreted in various ways,[2] but it would seem that its import should not be minimized. In any case it explains the scene in Acts 21.28, where the Apostle Paul was accused of

---

[1] One was found in 1871 fixed in the wall of a cloister; see Clermont-Ganneau in *Revue Archéologique*, 1872, pp. 214-34, 290-6, Pl. X. The other came to light in the course of excavations carried out by the Palestine Department of Antiquities in 1936; see *QDAP*, VI (1936) pp. 1-3. The first is now at Stamboul, and there is a cast of it in the Louvre; see René Dussaud, *Les monuments palestiniens et judaïques*, pp. 25-7; Vincent, in *RB*, 1921, p. 263, n. 1 and Pl. IV.

[2] According to Dalman, *op. cit.*, p. 376, 'this does not mean that the trespasser would be executed by the sentence of a court, but that, if the infuriated people killed him, it would be his own fault'. E. Bikerman, in *JQR*, XXXVII (1947), pp. 387-405, considers that only a legal penalty was implied.

having 'brought Greeks into the Temple', thus profaning the holy place. Even if Trophimus of Ephesus had the right to enter the court of the Gentiles, he was not permitted to go any farther.

Within the barrier, the holy place was divided into distinct areas reserved respectively, from east to west, for women, men, and, finally, priests. This inner court was built on a terrace, circled by walls and entered by nine gates: four on the north, four on the south, and one on the east side. This last was undoubtedly the most imposing. On account of its high doors of bronze imported from Corinth, it was known as the 'Corinthian Gate'[1] It may well be that gate which is referred to in Acts 3.2 as the 'Beautiful Gate', where the crippled man had been placed so that he could beg for alms 'from those who *went into* the sanctuary'. He was thus engaged when Peter and John were 'about to *go into* the Temple' (v. 3).

This gate, like all the others, was approached by a flight of five steps. In ordinary times these entrances were open, but in the event of any trouble they could quickly be closed. This was what happened, for instance, when the Apostle Paul narrowly escaped lynching at the hands of his fellow countrymen (Acts 21.30).[2]

[1] Watzinger, II, *op. cit.*, p. 41, identifies this with the Nicanor Gate, which the present author places elsewhere.

[2] A large staff, with officers (Luke 22.4, 52), under the orders of a commander (Acts 4.1, 5.24–26), was employed to guard and keep order in the Temple.

The first section of the inner court was called 'the women's court', not because men were excluded from it, but because women, no doubt for reasons connected with ritual purity, could not go any farther in.

According to the Mishna, a number of small unroofed rooms had been made here for storing wine, oil, and wood. Between these rooms were thirteen chests or coffers, in the form of inverted trumpets, in which offerings for the expenses of the Temple services were placed. It was here that the poor widow brought the two mites 'of her poverty' (Mark 12.41-4) when Jesus saw her. It is recorded that he was sitting there, and it is possible, therefore, that stone benches were placed against the walls. It was in this place also that Jesus sometimes taught, and declared himself to be 'the light of the world' (John 8.12-20).[1]

The 'men's court', or the 'court of Israel', formed the second section (187 × 135 cubits). It was raised 15 steps, perhaps 3 m. 75 cm., above the women's court and was entered by six gates, three on the north and three on the south, and by a seventh opening from the women's court. This gate was one of the most important in the Temple, and Father Abel identifies

---

[1] The place is called 'The Treasury', but since the Treasury, properly speaking, was not open to the public, most commentators agree that the word 'in' should be understood to mean 'near'. Thus Lagrange, *Évangile selon Saint Jean*, p. 235. See also *Bible du Centenaire, Le Nouveau Testament*, p. 155, n. *e*.

it with the Nicanor[1] Gate, so-called after the Jew who had presented its gold and silver doors. Several of the episodes described in the Gospels may have taken place there. It was, perhaps, the scene of the 'presentation' of Jesus by Joseph and Mary (Luke 2.22), and it may have been here that the publican of the parable stood (Luke 18.13). Moreover, women and others who did not wish to go farther in could see, through its wide arch, what was happening in the priests' court, especially in the immediate vicinity of the altar.

Jews who were in a state of ceremonial purity assembled in the men's court at the times when the rites were being celebrated, either to pray or to be present at the offering of the sacrifice. The indications given by the Evangelist Luke are thus quite accurate, for example: 'While all the people were *outside*, at prayer, at the time of the offering [of incense].[2] The people then were in the 'court of Israel'. Nevertheless they had the right, on occasions, to pass the boundary of the priests' court (a stone

[1] E. Wiesenberg, 'The Nicanor Gate', *Journal of Jewish Studies*, III No. 7 (1952) pp. 14–29; Dussaud in *Syria*, VI (1295) p. 99; Roussel in *Revue des Etudes Grecques*, 1934, p. 79. The burial-place of the Nicanor family was discovered at the Mount of Olives. An ossuary bears an inscription stating that it contains 'the bones of the son of Nicanor the Alexandrian who made the gates', *PEF.QS*, 1903, pp. 125 and 326. Quoted by Abel, *Histoire de la Palestine*, II, p. 377, n. 1. North, in *Orientalia*, 24 (1955) p. 341, takes this to refer to the doors of the tomb.

[2] The offering of incense was carried out in the *hekâl* on a special altar; see below, p. 95.

balustrade 1 cubit high). At the Feast of Tabernacles
the faithful did in fact enter the priests' court to
walk seven times round the altar while the high-
priest sprinkled it with water. It was on such an
occasion that Jesus said: 'He who believes in me,
out of his belly shall flow streams of living water, as
the Scripture says' (John 7.38).[1] This saying recalls
in a most striking and remarkable way the symbolism
of Mesopotamia and the theme of the 'flowing bowl.'[2]

The altar of burnt offerings was directly in a line
with the gate opening into the women's court and
opposite the entrance to the Temple.[3] It was built
of undressed stone and most probably occupied the
site of the rock of Ornan. It was approached from
the south, not by a stair but by a ramp.[4] A laver

[1] There is no reference here to any particular text. The *Bible du
Centenaire* suggests that 'the text alluded to was perhaps taken from
a book which has been lost', n. *e* to John 7.38. The evidence in
Lagrange, *Évangile selon Saint Jean*, p. 216, is equally negative. The
passage which most closely resembles it is Isa. 58.11.

[2] So far as the author is aware, no commentator has noted this
resemblance, further reference to which will be made below. Baumgartner, in a personal communication has however pointed out that
two scholars have in fact noticed this: see M. Burrows, *What Mean
These Stones* (1941), p. 264; R. Bultmann, *Das Evangelium des
Johannes* (1939), p. 229.

[3] On one occasion Jesus reminded the Pharisees of the blood of
Zachariah, son of Barachiah, who was killed 'between the sanctuary
and the altar' (Matt. 23.35). The site is thus exactly indicated; the
distance between the sanctuary and the altar was 11 m.

[4] The dimensions given by various writers differ. According to
Josephus, the base of the altar was 25 m. square, and its height was
7 m. 50 cm. In the Mishna the altar is rectangular ($30 \times 30 \times 5$
cubits), resting on a rimmed socket ($32 \times 32 \times 1$ cubits).

(*kiyor*) was placed between the vestibule of the Temple and the place of sacrifice. The sacrificial beasts were tethered to twenty-four rings and slaughtered on the north side of the altar on which they were to be burnt. The fire was fed with fig-, walnut- or pine-wood; never olive-wood. The blood was poured on to the lower part of the altar, whence it was carried away through holes pierced in the stone, it was said, as far as the Kidron.[1] All this was carried out to an accompaniment of singing, blowing of trumpets, and prostrations.

The Temple. Herod, in his zeal, adhered to the arrangement laid down by Solomon, although he enriched it after the Greek manner. It was divided, therefore, into three parts: *ulâm* (portico or porch), *hekâl* (holy place), *debîr* (most holy place) (fig. XXI).[2]

The porch (*ulâm*), which was approached by twelve steps, consisted of a façade 100 cubits (50 m.) wide and 100 cubits in height. In the centre was a great doorway, 40 cubits high and 20 cubits wide. It is possible that, on the model of some hellenistic buildings, there was a triangular[3] pediment above

[1] Mishna, *Middoth*, III, 2 and 3; Mishna, *Yoma*, V, 6; de Vogüé, *Le Temple de Jérusalem*, pp. 26-7. There is, however, some reason for doubt in this matter, according to Father Lagrange, *RB*, 1911, p. 411.

[2] The Mishna preserves some detailed measurements, which differ in certain respects from those given by Josephus and are generally to be preferred. On this point, Watzinger's suggested reconstruction is followed here.

[3] As on some of the temple-tombs of Petra, for example.

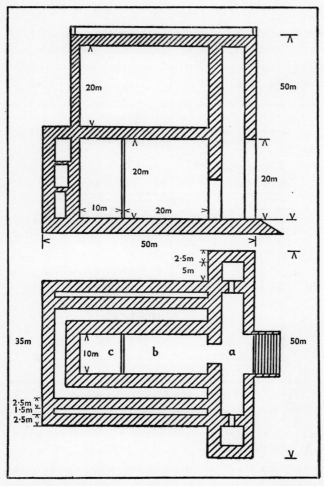

XXI. The Temple of Herod. Reconstruction: Ground plan and vertical section (from Watzinger, Denkmäler Palästinas)

the doorway surmounted at one time by an eagle with outspread wings,[1] and that the façade was completed by a colonnade supporting an upper story (fig. XXII).

XXII. The Temple of Herod. Reconstruction: The Façade (from Watzinger, op. cit., II, Pl. 7)

The way into the holy place was through a door with two (or four) leaves, over which hung a curtain of woollen material embroidered with a map of the heavens. The door was 20 cubits high and 10 cubits

[1] This was the eagle to which the more rigorist Jews objected.

wide,[1] and the lintel was decorated with golden vine leaves.[2] The holy place (*hekâl*) was 40 cubits long, 20 cubits wide, and 40 cubits high.[3] There is no information about its decoration, but it is known that the altar of incense stood in the centre with the table of shewbread on the left and the seven-branched lampstand on the right.[4]

The holy place was divided from the holy of holies, not by a wall, as in Solomon's Temple, but by a double curtain.[5] It was this curtain which was torn from top to bottom on the afternoon of Good Friday at the moment when Jesus expired (Mark 15.38;

[1] Abel (*op. cit.*, p. 377) gives different measurements: the height of the entrance, 25 m. 41 cm.; width, 7 m. 39 cm.

[2] A type of decoration found in many Eastern temples; one of the best examples is that of Qanawat at Djebel Druze.

[3] Abel, *op. cit.*, p. 378, gives the height of the *hekâl* as 27 m. 72 cm.

[4] See Daniélou, *op. cit.*, p. 62, quoting Philo: 'One must not omit to mention that, of the three objects in the holy place—the lamp-stand, the table, the altar of incense—one, the altar, expresses symbolically thanksgiving for the material elements; the table symbolizes thanksgiving for everything in the earthly order, the lampstand expresses thanksgiving for the whole heavenly order, so that no part of the cosmos may be guilty of ingratitude, but every part of the world may give thanks, each material element and all activities not only on earth but also in heaven.' According to Josephus, the lampstand had 'as many branches as the number of the planets, including the sun'.

[5] According to Josephus, the curtain was woven in four colours, symbolizing the four elements. Philo offers, as an alternative inter-pretation, the following: the veil represents the air which divides the unchanging heavens from the sublunary regions which are subject to change. Cf. Daniélou, *op. cit.*, p. 63. According to Rabbi Josiah, there was only one veil. Cf. Vincent in *RB*, 1954, p. 31.

Matt. 17.51). The holy of holies was completely empty; only the high priest was allowed to enter it on the Day of Atonement.

Like the first Temple, the whole building was encased in a number of small rooms—thirty-eight in all—forming three stories and rising to a height of 40 cubits (20 m.).[1] Above the whole sanctuary (*hekâl+debîr*) and equal to it in area there was a large room, the purpose of which is not known; its flat roof was 100 cubits above the level of the lower rooms and matched the height of the porch. The whole edifice was designed to present an appearance of grandeur while conforming as closely as possible to religious tradition.

Built of snow-white stone, embellished with panels of gold, the roof studded with gilded pinnacles,[2] Herod's Temple was indeed one of the wonders of Jerusalem.[3] It is easy to understand the admiration with which it was regarded by the people of those days, who used indeed to swear by the gold of the Temple (Matt. 33.16). It was the symbol of a power believed to be invincible, and to many it must have seemed a token of enduring national prosperity.

---

[1] In Solomon's Temple, 15 cubits (7 m. 50 cm.).

[2] To prevent birds from perching there and soiling it.

[3] Overall size: 100 cubits (50 m.); width of the façade, 100 cubits; at the back, 54 cubits (27 m.); height, 100 cubits. The interior dimensions of Notre Dame in Paris are 130×48×35 metres (427× 160×115 ft.).

But the fate which overtook it is now common knowledge. After a brief period of pseudo-independence, Palestine was to experience, under the Roman procurators, an administration which became increasingly rigid and vigilant. At the times of the great feasts, when the population of the city was swollen by the concourse of pilgrims and more liable to be roused to fanatical excitement, with a consequent risk of serious disturbances, the procurator would move into Jerusalem from his official residence at Caesarea. Father Vincent and other scholars find reasons for believing that he occupied the fortress of Antonia at the north-western angle of the Temple precincts, from which he could keep under observation the masses who crowded into the Temple courts. From this point also he could, if necessary, intervene with the least possible delay.[1] It has been suggested, therefore, that Pilate held his tribunal in a paved court[2] in the fortress of Antonia, and that Jesus appeared before him there.[3] Thus this whole great mass of buildings would be the starting point of the *via dolorosa* whose goal was Golgotha.[4]

*　　　　*　　　　*

[1] There was direct communication, by two separate stairways, between Antonia and each of the two porches (see fig. XX). Abel, *Histoire de la Palestine*, I, p. 374.

[2] The *lithostratos* of John 19.13.

[3] Father Vincent, *Jérusalem de l'Ancien Testament*, I, pp. 216-21.

[4] This question will be discussed in detail in a later volume in this series, *Golgotha and the Church of the Holy Sepulchre*.

As Jesus had foretold, the evil days came when the city, surrounded by trenches, besieged and beleaguered on all sides, was to be destroyed so that not one stone remained upon another.[1] A general insurrection broke out in A.D. 66, and the Romans, having reduced the provinces to subjection, methodically laid siege to Jerusalem. An increasingly severe blockade made resistance hopeless, and the two factions which strove for power in the city made the disaster inevitable. Simon Bar Giora commanded the sector of the upper city, John of Giscala defended the Temple precincts. In May A.D. 70 the assault began. Titus gained possession of Antonia in July, not without difficulty, but the Zealots who occupied the sanctuary refused to surrender. In August the Romans ruthlessly set fire to all the woodwork of the Temple.[2] A soldier flung a torch into one of the side-rooms, which immediately caught fire, and the flames spread rapidly. Titus managed to salvage a few objects from the Temple furnishings and these were displayed at his Triumph: the seven-branched lampstand, the golden table of shewbread, and the sacred horns were later reproduced in one of the reliefs on the triumphal arch which was erected in Rome after the death of the victorious general (see the illustration on the cover of the present volume).

So the third Temple was destroyed by fire and

[1] Luke, 19.43-4; Mark, 12.2.

[2] For details see Abel, *Histoire de la Palestine*, II, p. 34.

again the sacrifices came to an end. There was a time, during the second Jewish revolt, when Simon bar Cochba,[1] leader of the rebels, occupied Jerusalem (A.D. 132) and it seemed as if the Temple might

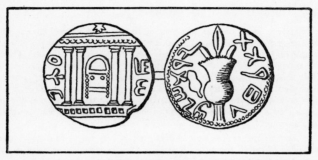

XXIII. Coin of Bar Cochba with Representation of the Temple (from Vincent and Abel, Jérusalem nouvelle, II, p. 885)

rise again from its ruins. Bar Cochba even had the audacity to strike coins bearing on them the image of the Temple (fig. XXIII). But his success was brief. The Romans returned in force and crushed the revolt completely. Jerusalem became a pagan city, Colonia Aelia Capitolina. The Temple was obliterated and on its site were erected, face to face, the statues of Hadrian the Conqueror and Jupiter

[1] Traces of this celebrated rebel have appeared in the Dead Sea Scroll in a striking autograph document in which the name is written 'Sim'on ben Koseba'. See *RB*, 1953, pp. 276-94.

Capitolinus, the god who had given him the victory.[1]
This was the final end of the Temple of Yahweh.
When, in A.D. 333, the pilgrim of Bordeaux visited
Jerusalem, he was shown the desolate rock on which
each year the assembled Jews poured oil, lamenting
and rending their garments.[2]

[1] After a very careful analysis of the texts, Father Vincent, in
Jérusalem Nouvelle, II, pp. 15-19, considers that there was no actual
temple of Jupiter on the site of the Jewish sanctuary. Father Abel,
Histoire de la Palestine, II, p. 100, suggests that 'it is not improbable
that a small pagan building was erected on the site at present
occupied by the Dome of the Chain outside the pierced rock to
which Jewish visitors were admitted once a year to mourn, and which
permitted a view of the remains of the house of God as a witness and
an example'.

[2] '*Sunt ubi et statuae duae Adriani, est et non longe de statuas lapis
pertusus; ad quem veniunt Judaei singulis annis et unguent eum et lamentant
se cum gemitu et vestimenta sua scindunt et sic recedunt.*'

V

THE HARAM ESH-SHERIF

It would be impossible to give in a few pages an account of all the buildings which have occupied the Temple site from the time of the destruction at the hands of Hadrian (A.D. 135) to the present day. But the visitor to Jerusalem today might well wish to have some idea of the successive stages in the history of this most sacred place.[1] Here the three monotheistic religions of the world claim a common past in which each, in its different way, sought the one true God.

From the evidence of the Fathers,[2] it seems that the Jews were forbidden, by official decree, to enter Jerusalem. According to Origen, however, it was tacitly admitted that from time to time they might go into the precincts of the former Temple to mourn and offer prayers there.

[1] There is a systematic and well documented account of this history in Vincent and Abel, *Jérusalem nouvelle*, II, pp. 875-1004. On the Moslem Haram there is a brief description in *Notice illustrée sur Al-Haram al-Sharif*, *Jérusalem*, published by the Conseil superieur islamique.

[2] Justin and Tertullian, for example.

By the time of Constantine and the Byzantine Emperors (fourth century) the Christians had returned to favour, but the Emperor, after his conversion, was more intent on honouring Christian relics than on restoring Jewish monuments. To him, therefore, were due the 'Constantine trilogy', dedicated to the Nativity (Bethlehem), the Resurrection (*Anastasis* = Holy Sepulchre), and the Ascension (*Eleona*).

It is not surprising that in A.D. 362 Julian the Apostate authorized the Jews, as a challenge to Christianity, to rebuild the Temple. But at his death, the project, which had not advanced very far, was abandoned.

The time of the Empress Eudocia (fifth century) saw a revival of the Christian passion for building. A considerable part at least of the Golden Gate[1] and the decoration of the Double Gate[2] date from that epoch.

The capture of Jerusalem by the Persians (A.D. 614) marked the end of the Byzantine age and the beginning of a new time of troubles. After 627, and the brief revival of Byzantium, a new power, that of Islam, came on the scene. In A.D. 638 the Caliph Omar occupied Jerusalem. His principal objective was to recover relics of Mahomet, of whom it was

[1] Father Abel, *op. cit.*, p. 911, places the Beautiful Gate mentioned in Acts 3.2, here. But the author prefers a different identification: see above, p. 83.

[2] See above, p. 82.

said that, 'carried on his winged mare el-Bouraq, and accompanied by the Angel Gabriel, he came, after one night's riding, to the sanctuary of Jerusalem where Abraham, Moses and Jesus awaited him.'[1]

Undeterred by the pitiable condition in which he found the holy place, Omar took the lead in the work of clearance, carrying the earth away in the skirt of his gown. Then, turning towards Mecca, he and his companions pronounced the ritual prayer: the holy place of the Jews became Moslem soil (fig. XXIV). A temporary mosque was soon erected on the southern sector of the Haram, on the site where later the El-Aqsa Mosque was to stand. This was the work of Wahd (A.D. 705-15), but it was not completed until 780.

His father Abd-el-Melik, fifth of the Umayyad Caliphs, had planted on the sacred rock a smaller mosque, octagonal in plan, the *Qubbet es-Sakhra* (Dome of the Rock) erroneously called the Mosque of Omar. It was begun in A.D. 687 and completed, in essentials, in 691.

But the Moslem domination was to suffer eclipse. In July 1099 the Crusaders entered Jerusalem and the Mosque became a Christian church, the *Templum Domini* (fig. XXV). An altar dedicated to St Nicholas was set up on the rock, which in 1162 was encircled by a wrought-iron grille. King Baldwin occupied El-Aqsa, but his rule was brief. After the defeat of the

[1] Vincent and Abel, *op. cit.*, p. 932.

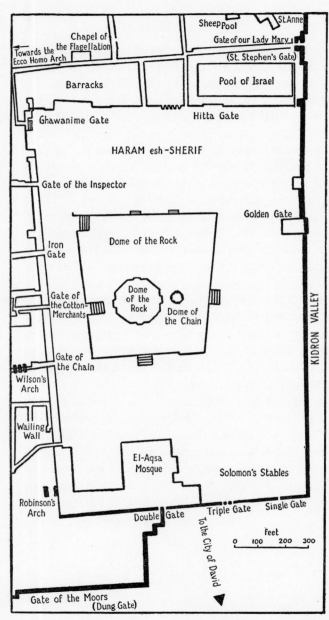

XXIV. Plan of Haram esh-Sherif (from Vincent and Abel, op. cit., Pl. III.

Franks at Hattin in Galilee on July 4, 1187, the final
outcome was not in doubt; on September 20, 1187,
Saladin arrived beneath the walls of Jerusalem.
When negotiations for an honourable settlement had

XXV. Seals of Baldwin I and the Knights Templar
(a) *Above the wall, the Holy Sepulchre, the Tower of*
David, the Dome of the Rock
(b) *The Dome of the Rock surmounted by the Cross*
(Vincent and Abel, op. cit., pp. 945, 971)

failed, one of the Palestine barons, Balian d'Ibelin,
addressed the Sultan in desperation: 'We shall slay
our sons and our daughters, we shall burn the city
and overthrow the Temple and all the sanctuaries
which are also your sanctuaries'.[1] Finally an
arrangement was arrived at and, by payment of
ransom, several thousand people were released. The
Moslems reoccupied Jerusalem. The chronicler Ibn
al-Athir has described one of the most dramatic

[1] See René Grousset, *L'epopée des croisades*, p. 248.

incidents: the cross which the Crusaders had erected on the 'Mosque of Omar' was thrown down before the army of Saladin and in the presence of the Frankish population. When it fell, the whole multitude gave a great cry. The Moslems shouted: 'Great is Allah!' The Franks gave utterance to their grief. So great was the clamour that it seemed as if the very earth shook.[1]

Saladin immediately put in hand the necessary repairs. He covered the exterior walls of the *Qubbet es-Sakhra* with mosaics, restored the interior decoration with inlaid plaster, and placed an inscription above the gallery. He also adorned El-Aqsa with magnificent mosaics and placed there the carved wooden throne (*minbar*) which had been made twenty years before at Aleppo according to the instructions of Nur-eddin.

Another great restoration was carried out by Soliman the Magnificent (A.D. 1520-66), who replaced the mosaics on the outside of *Qubbet es-Sakhra* by enamelled tiles from Tabriz in Persia (Pl. 7). He also had lattice windows made, filled with coloured glass, which admit a subdued and diffuse light. When the eye of the visitor becomes accustomed to the dimness, it is possible to see the remarkable mosaics in the aisles, which date from the eighth century and display designs of palm-trees, sprays of foliage, garlands of flowers and fruits,

[1] Ibid., p. 252.

bunches of grapes. The effect is all the more striking by contrast with the bare rock, whose rugged mass, visible beyond the iron grille of the Crusaders, throws into relief the delicate tapestries of stone endowing them with a quality which the most skilful craftsmen could not have achieved intentionally.

On this area of about 145,000 square metres, of which the Mosque of the rock occupies only a small section, stand a number of less important buildings: *Qubbet es-Silsile* (Dome of the Chain); arcades known as *Mawazine* (scales), because it is said that at the Last Judgement the scales in which good and evil shall be weighed will hang there; fountains, including that of the Sultan Mameluk Qaitbay; the throne of Burhan-eddin, etc.; and these various monuments are interspersed with the darkness of tall cypresses, recalling the fact that this is a high place, where, from time immemorial, the Semitic peoples have worshipped beneath sacred trees.

In the course of this study it has been made plain that, twice over, the words of Jesus have come to pass; and of the Temple which was the pride of Solomon and of Herod the Great, and the treasured possession of the chosen people, not 'one stone has been left upon another'. But in the face of this scene of desolation and decay one may recall that other saying, portentous but nevertheless pregnant with hope: 'Heaven and earth shall pass away, but my words shall not pass away.'

SHORT BIBLIOGRAPHY

Only standard works and important articles are included, and of the latter only the most recent.

Excavations

R. Dussaud, 'Des fouilles à entreprendre sur l'emplacement du Temple de Jérusalem', in *RHR.*, LXXIX, 1919, pp. 1-9.

Warren, *Underground Jerusalem* . . . (1876), with a volume of plates (1867-70).

Wilson and Warren, *The Recovery of Jerusalem*: A Narrative of Exploration and Discovery in the City and the Holy Land, 2 vols (1871).

History

Rev. Father Abel, *Histoire de la Palestine*, I-II (1952).

L. Desnoyers, *Histoire du peuple hébreu des Juges à la Captivité*, III (1930).

M. Noth, *Histoire d'Israël* (1954).

G. Ricciotti, *Histoire d'Israël*, I-II (1939).

E. Schürer, *Geschichte des jüdischen Volkes im Zeitaller Jesu Christi* (1909).

Textbooks and General Works

W. F. Albright, *Archaeology and the Religion of Israel* (1942; third edition, 1953).

G. Barrois, *Manuel d'archéologie biblique*, II (1953).

I. Benzinger, *Hebräische Archäologie* (1927).

G. Dalman, *Les itinéraires de Jésus* (1930).

Dictionnaire encyclopédique de la Bible, II (undated).

K. Galling, *Biblisches Reallexikon* (1937).

H. Gressmann, *Altorientalische Texte und Bilder zum Alten Testament* (1926).

F. J. Hollis, *The Archaeology of Herod's Temple* (1934).

Fr. Michaeli, 'Le Temple et la Loi' (1953) (unpublished thesis).

K. Moehlenbrink, *Der Tempel Salomos* (1932).

Bibliography

G. Perrot and Ch. Chipiez, *Histoire de l'Art dans l'Antiquité*, IV, pp. 159-338 (1887).

F. de Saulcy, *Jérusalem* (1882).

J. Simons, *Jerusalem in the Old Testament* (1952).

Rev. Father Vincent and Rev. Father Abel, *Jérusalem*, II (1926).

—— and Rev. Father Stève, *Jérusalem de l'Ancien Testament*, I (1954).

M. de Vogüé, *Le Temple de Jérusalem* (1864).

C. Watzinger, *Denkmäler Palästinas*, I-II (1933-5).

Articles and Specialist Studies

W. F. Albright, 'Two Cressets from Marisa and the Pillars of Jachin and Boaz', in *BASOR*, 85 (1942), pp. 18-27.

—— 'What were the Cherubim?' in *BA*, I, (1938), pp. 1-3.

A. Alt, 'Verbreitung und Herkunft des Syrischen Tempeltypus', in *Kleine Schriften*, II, pp. 100-115.

E. Bikerman, 'Une proclamation séleucide relative au Temple de Jérusalem', in *Syria*, XXV (1946-8), pp. 67-85.

S. A. Cook, 'The Age of Zerubbabel', in *Studies in Old Testament Prophecy*, pp. 19-36 (1950).

S. Corbett, 'Some Observations on the Gateways to the Herodian Temple in Jerusalem' in *PEQ*, 84, (1952) pp. 7-15.

J. Daniélou, 'La symbolique cosmique du Temple de Jérusalem', in *Symbolisme cosmique et monuments réligieux*, pp. 61-4 (1953).

Dhorme and Vincent, 'Les Chérubins,' in *RB*, 1926, pp. 328-58), 481-95.

K. Elliger, in *Geschichte und Altes Testament* 1953 (Festschrift A.Alt), on the Temple of Ezekiel.

P. L. Garber, 'Reconstructing Solomon's Temple', in *BA*, XIV, 1 (1951), pp. 2-24.

—— 'A Reconstruction of Solomon's Temple' in *Archaeology*, 5, pp. 165-72.

J. de Groot, *Die Altäre des Salomonischen Tempelhofs* (1924).

Mgr. L. Gry, 'La ruine du Temple par Titus', in *RB* (1948), pp. 215-26.

J. Jeremias, 'Das westliche Südtor des herodianischen Tempels', in *ZDPV*, 65, pp. 112-21.

Rev. Father Lagrange, 'Comment s'est formée l'enceinte du Temple de Jérusalem', in *RB*, 1893, pp. 90-113.

A. Lods, 'Les cuisines du Temple de Jérusalem', in *RHR*, CXXVII (1944), pp. 30-54.

H. G. May, 'The two Pillars before the Temple of Solomon', in *BASOR*, 88 (1942), pp. 19-27.

The Temple of Jerusalem

J. L. Myres, 'King Solomon's Temple and other Buildings and Works of Art', in *PEQ*, 1948, pp. 14-41.

M. B. Rowton, 'The Date of the Founding of Solomon's Temple' in *BASOR*, 119 (1950), pp. 20-2.

E. Schmidt, *Solomon's Temple in the Light of other Oriental Temples* (1902).

H. Schmidt, *Der heilige Fels in Jerusalem* (1933).

R. B. Y. Scott, 'The Pillars Jachin and Boaz', in *JBL*, LVIII (1939), pp. 143 *et seq.*

Rev. Father de Vaux, 'Les décrets de Cyrus et de Darius sur la reconstruction du Temple', in *RB*, 1937, pp. 29-57.

Rev. Father Vincent, 'La description du Temple de Salomon. Notes exégétiques sur I Rois VI', in *RB*, 1907, pp. 515-42.

—— 'Jérusalem', in *Dictionnaire de la Bible*, Supplément XXI, cols, 897-966 (1948).

—— 'L'autel des holocaustes et le caractère du Temple d'Ezéchiel', in *Analecta Bollandiana* (1949).

—— 'Le temple hérodien d'après la Mishnah', in *RB*, 1954, pp. 5-35 (to be continued).

C. Virolleaud, 'Sur l'idole de la jalousie du Temple de Jérusalem (Ez. viii, 3-5),' in *RES* (1942-45), pp. 59-63.

L. Waterman, 'The Damaged "Blueprints" of the Temple of Solomon', in *JNES*, II (1947), pp. 284-94.

—— 'The Treasuries of Solomon's Private Chapel', in *JNES*, VI (1947), pp. 161-3.

—— 'A Rebuttal' in *JNES*, VII (1948), pp. 54-5.

G. E. Wright, 'Solomon's Temple Resurrected', in *BA*, IV (1941), pp. 17-31.

—— 'The Temple of Solomon', in *BA*, VII (1944), pp. 73-7.

—— 'Dr Waterman's View concerning the Solomonic Temple', in *JNES*, VII (1948), pp. 53-5.

—— 'The Stevens Reconstruction of the Solomonic Temple' in *BA*, XVIII (1955), pp. 41-4.

C. C. Wylie, 'On King Solomon's Molten Sea', in *BA*, XII (1949), pp. 86-90.

Monographs and Studies on the Ark

W. R. Arnold, *Ephod and Ark* (1917).

K. Budde, *Die Lade Jahves* (1906).

M. Dibelius, *Die Lade Jahves* (1906).

H. Gressmann, *Die Lade Jahves und das Allerheiligste des Salomonischen Tempels* (1920).

Bibliography

H. Gunkel, *Die Lade Jahves, ein Thronsitz* (1906).

R. Hartmann, 'Zelt und Lade', in *ZATW*, 37 (1917), pp. 225-34.

E. Klamroth, *Lade und Tempel*.

G. H. May, 'The Ark. A Miniature Temple', in *AJSL*, LII (1936), pp. 215-34.

J. Morgenstern, *The Ark, the Ephod and the Tent of Meeting* (1945).

N. H. Tur-Sinai, 'The Ark of God at Beit Shemesh . . .', in *Vetus Testamentum*, I (1951), pp. 275-86.

Moslem Monuments

M. van Berchem, *The Mosaics of the Dome of the Rock at Jerusalem* (1932).

K. A. C. Creswell, *The Origin of the Plan of the Dome of the Rock* (1924).

Illustrated Note on Al Haram al-Sharif, Jerusalem (1924).

M. T. Lagrange, 'La prétendue violation de la mosquée d'Omar', in *RB*, 1911, 440-2.

E. T. Richmond, *The Dome of the Rock in Jerusalem* (1924).

The Temple and the Psalms

No discussion of the use of the Psalms in the Temple has been attempted. This is a literary and exegetical rather than an archaeological question, and is obviously related to the history of religions. It is certain that pilgrims and others of the faithful recited the Psalms in the Temple. It is probable, also, that at the annual ceremonies Yahweh was 'enthroned' as king. On all these points reference may be made to A. R. Johnson, 'The Psalms', in *The Old Testament and Modern Study*, ed. H. H. Rowley, 1951.

Recent studies on the subject are:

S. Mowinckel, *Zum israelitischen Neujahr und zur Deutung der Thronbesteigungs-psalmen* (1952).

—— '*Der achtundsechzigste Psalm* (1953).

J. de Fraine, *L'aspect religieux de la royauté israélite* (1954).

A. R. Johnson, *Sacral Kingship in Ancient Israel* (1955).

KEY TO ABBREVIATIONS OF
JOURNALS

AJSL   American Journal of Semitic Languages and Literatures.
BA   The Biblical Archaeologist.
BASOR   Bulletin of the American Schools of Oriental Research.
JBL   Journal of Biblical Literature.
JNES   Journal of Near Eastern Studies.
PEQ formerly PEF.QS Palestine Exploration Quarterly.
RB   Revue Biblique.
RHR   Revue de l'histoire des Religions.
ZATW   Zeitschrift für die alttestamentliche Wissenschaft.
ZDPV   Zeitschrift des deutschen Palästinavereins.